Dad Cooks Up a Party

Dad Cooks Up a Party

The Complete Guide to Entertaining Family and Friends

Bob Sloan

Illustrations by Steven Guarnaccia

Macmillan• USA

MACMILLAN
A Simon & Schuster Macmillan Company
1633 Broadway
New York, NY 10019

MACMILLAN is a registered trademark of Macmillan, Inc.

Library of Congress Cataloging-in-Publication Data

Sloan, Bob.
     Dad cooks up a party / Bob Sloan; illustrations by Steven Guarnaccia
        p. cm.
     Includes index.
     ISBN 0-02-860385-0
     1. Cookery. 2. Entertaining. 3. Menus. I. Title.
TX714.S588   1996
642' .4—dc20   96-4112   CIP

Design by Amy Peppler Adams—designLab, Seattle

Manufactured in the United States of America

10 9 8 7 6 5 4 3 2 1

For my boys, Nate and Leo

Acknowledgments

My grandfather told me never to trust anyone who ate oysters with a fork, which is why I trust Susan Lescher implicitly and thank her for her guidance and counsel. I would also like to thank my editor, Justin Schwartz, a fellow dad, who wanted to see our kind more secure and confident in the kitchen.

Like many of my best ideas, this one emerged out of a conversation with Steven Guarnaccia. Gwynne Marshall tested many of these recipes, as did Lela Nargi, who also helped with some editing. Josh Eisen offered advice and corkscrew with some of the wine selections.

My friends Neal, Molly, Fred, Mary, Diane, and Jim were gracious enough to serve as guinea pigs to see if many of these parties worked. They owe me big time.

I thank the Sanfields and Izenbergs for their hospitality in Leelanau, Michigan, where much of this book was written, and the Bahles for their summer friendship. Also my folks for all their help.

Most of all I thank my wife Randi for her extraordinary advice and support and for doing the dishes.

The "Pizza" and "Halloween" chapters originally appeared in a slightly different form in *Family Life* magazine. The author wishes to thank them for their permission to use them here.

Contents

Introduction

Dad cooks. It's no longer an oxymoron. Dads are now in the kitchen more than ever before. Not just scrambling eggs and flipping pancakes, but baking, broiling, cooking fish in the frying pan, taking the meat loaf out of the oven. And now that he has a handle on making the basic three square meals, it's time for Dad to throw a party.

With courage and fortitude, Dad is going to cook for his friends, relatives, the guys whose threesome you joined at the local course last week. Get their addresses on some invitations, their wives and kids, too. You've got the oven preheated, the main course is marinating, and dessert is chilling in the fridge.

It's Showtime!

In this book I've given you not only recipes and tons of time-saving tips, but, what's equally important, suggested reasons to have a party. Don't wait for something as wan as an anniversary or a birthday or a kid's graduation. Get inventive and you can find all kinds of reasons for having people over for a meal. Invite your future in-laws over to dinner. Host a Caribbean feast as an excuse to do some limbo. Throw together some penne and sausage for 12 friends as a prelude to some serious charades. Slow-roast a barbecued brisket to serve the guys during the football game, knowing that after they taste it they'll be back again a week later. Or just get the family together for a festive morning of "breakfast specials" prepared by dad in his own inimitable style.

Measurement Chart

1 tablespoon = 3 teaspoons

2 tablespoons = 1/8 cup or 1 ounce

4 tablespoons = 1/4 cup

16 tablespoons = 1 cup

2 cups = 1 pint

2 pints = 1 quart

4 quarts = 1 gallon

Dad's Kitchen Homilies:

- If your wife wants to help, let her watch the kids.
- If the kids want to help, let them peel the potatoes.
- Garlic cooks quickly.
- If you expect to serve dinner on time, you can't forget to preheat the oven.
- If you cook, someone else should clean up.

Dad's Ten Commandments of Cooking

1. Read the recipe through entirely before you start. Try to conceptualize what you are about to do, gaining a feel for the culinary battleground before you start cooking.

2. Make sure you have all the ingredients on hand. Not just the big things, like the Thanksgiving turkey, but the little ones—a key spice, enough cooking oil, chicken broth. Nothing so easily sabotages a dish as getting halfway into a recipe and realizing you're missing something you need.

3. Assemble and prep all ingredients before starting to cook the dish. If you've ever wondered why the chef's on television cook with such ease, it's because everything they need to make the recipe is prepared ahead of time. Follow this commandment and you'll have your own show before you know it.

4. Make sure the pan is hot enough. Once the food is added, it absorbs the heat and cools down the pan. Household stoves don't have hot enough burners to maintain the heat. Therefore you need to place the pan on the heat and let it get hot before adding the ingredients.

5. Once you feel comfortable making a dish, do not be afraid to improvise within reason. This is how new recipes are born.

6. Wash all surfaces and knives that come in contact with raw chicken immediately with hot, soapy water to prevent salmonella contamination. Never cut a cooked chicken on the same cutting surface as a raw one without cleaning it first. Never serve marinade that raw chicken has soaked in—make a separate batch for use as a sauce.

7. Don't mess with the baking ingredients. The ratio of wet and dry ingredients, eggs and leavening agents, pan size, and baking time is all carefully calculated. If you vary them even slightly, it will throw off the recipe.

8. Stir batters for cakes and muffins only until they are just mixed together. Over-stirring will cause them to be dense.

9. Don't have an aneurysm trying to make everything yourself. If there's a bakery nearby that has fabulous apple pies, by all means get one for dessert. If the Italian deli has great homemade mozzarella, serve that as an appetizer. It's better to cook within your limits than to over-extend yourself and jeopardize the meal.

10. Trust yourself. If something is burning, take it out of the oven. If something isn't done enough, cook it some more. Oven temperatures and stovetop burners vary in heat, some pieces of chicken are thicker than others. These recipes will lead you to the cusp of culinary greatness, but you may have to use some of your own judgment to finish things off.

How To Read a Recipe

It's not a Dad thing to do, but you've got to find a way to read the whole recipe first before you start. I know instructions are only meant to be looked at as a last resort, after the thing you're assembling is scattered across the basement linoleum in hopeless chaos. But cooking is different from putting together a kid's wagon. Screws and wing nuts don't go anywhere if you abandon them in frustration for a night or a week. With cooking there's the *time factor*. People are coming for dinner and they expect to be fed. If they don't, they're liable to get touchy and take your autographed photo of Whitey Ford hostage until you come up with some grub.

So put your Dad-ness aside and follow these steps when addressing a recipe.

1. Read it through completely early enough so you have time to shop and order any ingredients you need.

2. Before you get started cooking, read it again.

3. Assemble all the ingredients and equipment on the counter. Preheat the oven, if necessary.

4. Prep, chop, slice, trim, or wash ingredients as noted in the ingredients list.

5. Start cooking.

Two Places at Once

Being a guest at your own party is not always going to be easy. You may find yourself making frequent trips crossing the great divide between the kitchen and the dining room. But I think you'll discover that far from feeling like a shirper on an Everest expedition, being the chef gives you a certain aura. Invite the boys into the kitchen. Tell them to bring their wine while you get the main course ready. Give them a sauce to stir, a pot to drain. Or if they're chicken, they can hop up on the counter like they did when they were kids and keep you company. Just make sure they don't find their way into the cabinets and eat all the cookies while you're busy at the stove and your back is turned.

Equipment

Food Processor

For chopping and making dough. The processor requires a delicate touch. An extra few seconds of processing or just 2 or 3 pulses too many and you can wind up pulverizing your ingredients to beyond what you need.

Blender

For pureeing soups and making drinks. When it comes to pureeing soups and sauces, the blender does a better job than the processor in making a smooth mixture.

Electric Hand Mixer

For egg whites, whipping mashed potatoes, and making cakes. I just got a cordless one of these and not having to clean the electrical cord after it's been draped in the batter is a big plus.

Casserole or Roasting Pan

For casseroles and other baked entrees. You should really have 2 stainless-steel, glass, or aluminum pans, one around 9x12-inch which handles 4 to 6 people and one 12x18-inch which handles 8 people.

10-inch Frying Pan

Every cook's most essential pan. You'll be using this in some capacity for almost every meal you make. I recommend one stainless steel and one cast iron.

3½-Quart Sauce Pan

For cooking vegetables, potatoes, rice, and other grains. It's also best to have 2 of these, in case you want to serve rice and steamed vegetables at the same meal.

Pasta Pot

For pasta and lobsters. Mandatory for many of these recipes and an essential contemporary kitchen tool as pasta is one of the most popular foods among kids today.

Baking Pan

For cookies and other baking needs. Two would be best. Mine are 12x18-inch with a ¾-inch lip. I prefer paying a little more and getting stainless steel rather than aluminum. Just make sure you dry them well before storing to keep the trays from rusting.

Wine Glass

Another key element in the kitchen, because most chefs know they cook a little better if they're sipping a glass of nice wine while they're working.

A Word About Pots

Quality pots and pans are not just for show. They really do work better. Without them it's like trying to hit a major league fast ball with the bats they give away at bat day. A heavy-bottomed pan will maintain and distribute the heat more evenly, especially if there is a layer of copper as well. I prefer the inside of my pans to be stainless-steel and the outsides either aluminum or stainless steel as well. But I am as equally attached to my cast-iron skillet as I am to my fancy pans and highly recommend you get a 10-inch one of your own, making sure to dry it well after each use so it doesn't get rusty on you.

Knives

Sharp knives are a dad's best friend in the kitchen. If you find you're doing a lot of cooking, you'll want to invest in an electric knife sharpener and go over the blades twice a year. You can help keep them sharp by not putting them in the dishwasher and not storing them loose in a drawer where the blades can bang around and become dull. Wash them by hand and use a knife block or magnetic bar to store them.

8-inch chef's knife—the most used knife in the kitchen, it handles all the chopping and slicing. After a while you'll be as handy with this as Rifleman Chuck Conners was with his Winchester.

4-inch paring knife—for small jobs. Very handy for trimming, peeling fruit, and getting into small places.

6-inch boning knife—for cutting up chickens, slicing meat and all those in-between kinds of slicing.

10-inch serrated knife—mostly for bread, but it also comes in handy on particularly delicate tomatoes

Cutting Board

You don't need one as large as you probably think you do. You'll find it's more useful to have two, each about 12x18 inches. There are designer cutting boards made from tempered glass. Do not use one of those. They're nearly impossible to chop on.

Other Utensils and Equipment

For the recipes in this cookbook you'll also need the following:

Loaf pans

Pie plates

9½-inch tube pan

Bundt pan

10-inch cake pan

Whisk

Rubber spatulas

2 large mixing bowls

2 medium mixing bowls

2 small mixing bowls

Melon baller

Nut crackers (for lobster)

Corkscrew

Big Bad Brunch

Recipes make 8 servings

I like brunch, although I admit for a time the word itself gave me a rash. I tried other monickers. "Let's meet for late breakfast." "How about an early lunch?" But brunch by any other name did not taste as sweet. It didn't have the same joyful connotation. Because even at its most overused, "brunch" still means lazy weekends, holidays, and sleeping late. It means a radical intake of comfort food, segueing, ideally, into a long nap.

Eleven o'clock is the perfect time to brunch. Any later, and the guests will be too hungry. Any earlier, and they'll have to rouse themselves from Sunday morning dreams of strolling along the Seine with Brigitte Bardot or Jean-Paul Belmondo and will be certain to resent you for it. A good brunch tip is to be sure to have coffee ready when your guests first arrive. Although these are friends, you might not have firsthand knowledge about how ornery they can be without their morning cup of joe.

MENU

Fresh O.J.
Mimosas
Bloody Marys
Scrapple from the Apple
Whitefish Salad
Wild Mushroom Frittata
Blueberry Sour Cream Coffee Cake

Fresh O.J.

Figure on 2 juice oranges per person. I sometimes add 1 pink grapefruit for every 8 oranges to make the juice a little more tart.

Mimosas

Makes 12 to 16 Drinks

This is the perfect way to make use of that bottle of sparkling wine someone from the office gave you several years ago for a now long-forgotten reason. Don't use real champagne for this drink; its subtlety will only be overwhelmed. You're better off investing in some freshly squeezed orange juice because that is what dictates the flavor.

1 bottle sparkling wine
1 quart orange juice, preferably
freshly squeezed and kept very cold

Fill a champagne flute half full with orange juice. Slowly fill the glass the rest of the way with the sparkling wine, tipping the glass slightly so that the wine eases down the side and doesn't foam up too much. Serve immediately.

MUSIC

Without a doubt, the Getz/Gilberto album, featuring "The Girl from Ipanema," is the quintessential brunch music. After all the Bossa Nova arrived on the scene right around the same time as brunch and fondue parties. Fortunately, the music and brunch have remained. Other albums contemporary with the birth of brunch are Brubeck's *Time Out*, Steisand's *Color Me Barbara*, and Dione Warwick's irrepressible *Valley of the Dolls*. I'm sure I spent more than one Sunday morning stuffing my face and snapping my fingers to "Do You Know the Way to San Jose?."

Bloody Marys

Makes 8 to 10 drinks

Some people have a couple of these instead of breakfast. Don't make them too strong or your guests will want to jump into your pool with their clothes on, whether you have a pool or not.

1 quart tomato juice
2 tablespoons Worcestershire sauce
1 tablespoon horseradish
1 teaspoon Tabasco
1 teaspoon salt

1 pinch celery seed (optional)
Ice
Vodka or gin
8 to 10 six-inch celery stalks (one for each drink)

1. Put the tomato juice, Worcestershire sauce, horseradish, tabasco, salt, and optional celery seed into a pitcher and stir together until combined.

2. To make each drink, fill an 8 to 10 ounce glass ⅔ full of ice. Pour in 4 ounces of tomato juice mix. Add 1 to 2 ounces of vodka, depending on how strong you want them, and stir well. Garnish with a celery stalk if desired.

drinks
Wine Selections

The following wines are suitable both for mimosas and to drink straight in case there's some left over. They all sell for around $10:

Mumm Cuvee Napa Brut "Prestige"
Piper Sonoma Brut
Michel Freres Blanc de Blancs
Codorniu Blanc de Blancs
Korbel "Brut"

Scrapple from the Apple

Makes 8 to 10 servings

Inspired by jazz great Charlie Parker's bop tune, this recipe is a riff on the traditional farm dish. The addition of the cooked apple gives it a touch of sweetness. Scrapple is a food that could become one of your signature dishes. Years later, when your kids compare notes with their college roommates about their parent's eccentricities, they can say, "Oh, but one thing my dad did do right was make this great thing for brunch called scrapple."

1 tablespoon butter

2 tart apples, such as Granny Smith or Macintosh, peeled, cored, and coarsely chopped

1 pound Italian sweet sausage or turkey sausage, removed from the casing

4 cups canned beef broth

1 cup yellow cornmeal

3 eggs

Note

You can make the scrapple up to one day in advance and then refrigerate it in the loaf pan. You also can make it up to three weeks in ad-vance and then freeze it. If you freeze the scrapple, let it thaw in the refrigerator for 24 hours. To reheat, cook slices of scrapple in a pan over medium heat for 3 to 4 minutes per side with 2 tablespoons of butter or in the microwave for 2 to 3 minutes on high.

1. Preheat the oven to 350°F. Generously grease a 4x9-inch loaf pan and line the bottom with waxed paper.

2. Place a large frying pan over medium-high heat. Add the butter. When it starts sizzling, spread it evenly so that it covers the bottom of the pan. Add the apple and cook, stirring frequently, until it is soft, about 4 minutes.

3. Add the sausage meat to the pan and cook, stirring frequently, until the sausage is cooked through and loses its pinkness, about 5 minutes. Transfer the sausage mixture to a strainer and let the fat drain off.

4. While the sausage is cooking, bring the beef broth to a boil in a large saucepan. When the broth comes to a boil, add the cornmeal in a slow, steady stream, stirring continuously. This helps alleviate lumps. Continue stirring until it is well combined. Return the mixture to a boil, and then reduce the heat to low and cook, uncovered, for 20 minutes, stirring frequently so that the mixture doesn't stick to the bottom.

5. Remove the mixture from the heat and stir in the sausage-apple mixture. Add the eggs and continue stirring until everything is well combined.

6. Transfer the mixture to the loaf pan, cover it tightly with aluminum foil, and bake it on the center rack of the oven for 50 minutes. Remove the aluminum foil and bake 20 minutes more or until a toothpick poked into the center comes out clean.

7. Remove the pan from the oven and let the scrapple cool for 5 minutes. Cut the loaf into 2-inch slices in the pan and remove them gently with a spatula.

Whitefish Salad

Makes 8 appetizer servings

If you live near Third Avenue Bagels in Manhattan or another such venerable deli, you might be able to buy this salad ready-made and save yourself a little time. If you can't, taking the few minutes to remove the bones from the whitefish yields the makings of an elegant contribution to this late-morning repast. And it'll taste good, too.

½ **large whitefish,**
    about 1½ pounds

2 scallions, chopped

½ **medium onion, chopped**

2 celery stalks, finely chopped

½ **cup sour cream**

1 tablespoon fresh lemon juice

1 tablespoon chopped fresh
    parsley

For serving

Pumpernickel bread

Lemon wedges

1. Pick the meat from the whitefish, being extremely careful to remove all the bones. After you have separated all the meat, discard the bones, and then pick through the meat one more time, flaking it with your fingers and looking for any small bones that might have slipped through.

2. Put the fish in a medium mixing bowl, add the rest of the ingredients, and stir together until they are well combined. Transfer the salad to a small serving bowl with a butter knife and serve with triangles of pumpernickel bread and small lemon wedges.

Note

You can make the whitefish salad the night before you serve it. Store it in the refrigerator in a well-sealed plastic container.

Wild Mushroom Frittata

Makes 8 servings

This is a type of quiche without the crust. It's got all the positive attributes of quiche, but you don't have to take the time to make the crust and you never actually have to say the word "quiche." You get to say "Frittata"—and drag it out, as if you really speak Italian. "Free-taaa-tah."

12 eggs

1 cup (½ pound) cheddar or gruyere cheese, grated

4 tablespoons (½ stick) butter

¾ pound shiitake or other wild mushrooms, stemmed and cut into thick slices

½ pound zucchini, rinsed and cut into ½-inch rounds

½ pound thinly sliced smoked ham, cut into 2-inch pieces

Note

Use a nonstick pan to cook the frittata. It will make it easier to remove it from the pan. If your pan doesn't have an ovenproof handle, wrap the handle in aluminum foil before putting the pan in the oven.

Frittata traditionally is served at room temperature. You can make yours up to an hour before the guests arrive. Simply cover the platter with aluminum foil until you are ready to serve it.

1. Preheat the oven to 425°F.

2. Beat the eggs in a mixing bowl. Add the grated cheese and stir to combine.

3. Place a 10-inch, oven-safe frying pan over medium-high heat. Add 2 tablespoons of the butter, and when it starts sizzling, spread evenly so that it covers the bottom of the pan. Add the mushrooms and zucchini slices and cook, stirring frequently, until the mushrooms are soft, about 6 minutes. Add the ham and cook 2 minutes more.

4. Increase the heat to high, add the remaining 2 tablespoons of butter, and spread it around the pan. Add the eggs and cheese mixture and cook, stirring continuously with a spatula, until the lower half of the eggs begins to set—about 1 minute. Be sure to incorporate the eggs around the edges of the pan when you are stirring.

5. Transfer the pan to the oven and cook until the frittata puffs slightly and is browned lightly on top, about 10 minutes.

6. Use a hot pad to remove the pan from the oven. Let it sit for a few minutes to set completely. Cut it into 8 slices, remove them from the pan with a flexible spatula, and arrange them in a circle on a large round platter. Garnish with some chopped parsley or chopped scallions.

Blueberry Sour Cream Coffee Cake

Makes 12 to 16 servings

The problem with this cake is that it is too rich and too delectable and too easy to prepare. The crucial thing here is to make sure that you have a real bundt pan. If you don't have one, get one, because you'll be getting requests for this cake from now on.

2 sticks (1/2 pound) butter at room temperature

2 cups granulated sugar

2 eggs

2¼ cups unbleached, all-purpose flour

1 tablespoon baking powder

1 pinch salt

1 pint sour cream

1 tablespoon vanilla extract

12 ounces frozen or 1 pint fresh blueberries

1. Preheat the oven to 350°F. Grease a 10-inch bundt pan and dust the inside lightly with flour.

2. Cream the butter and sugar together in a large mixing bowl with a wooden spoon until it makes a smooth mixture, about 2 minutes. Add the eggs one at a time, until they are fully incorporated into the mixture.

3. In a separate bowl, combine the flour, baking powder, and salt with a whisk until they are mixed together. Transfer the dry ingredients to the butter mixture and mix together.

4. Stir in the vanilla and the sour cream until they are incorporated. Add the blueberries and stir just until they are mixed into the batter.

5. Transfer the batter to the bundt pan, making sure that it is distributed evenly. The pan should be a little more than half full. Bake on the center rack for 1 hour or until a toothpick inserted in the center comes out clean. Let the cake cool for at least an hour before removing it from the pan.

Note

You can make the cake the day before you serve it. After removing it from the pan, let it cool completely before transferring it to a plate and covering it with plastic. You also can make this cake two weeks in advance; just let it cool completely before you wrap it carefully in plastic and then freeze it. Let the cake defrost overnight at room temperature.

You might have noticed that the food for this brunch can be made ahead of time, which should make your stretch run pretty calm. Everything can be set out on the table when the guests arrive. Remember to take the cake out of the freezer the night before if that's where you stored it.

TIP

To expedite the liberating of the cake from the pan, invert the pan over a serving plate and tap the bottom.

Breakfast at Dad's Diner

Recipes make 4 servings

Sometimes in the morning, before your kids are fully awake and have their complete wits (or lack of) about them, they may be vulnerable to a family-type experience, such as all of you eating together. That's the time to make them something special for breakfast. So get on your apron, Mr. Short-Order Dad, and one of those white paper caps, shove a cigarette in the corner of your mouth, and invite the family to Dad's Diner.

Most dads feel confident about cooking breakfast. The usual torpor that paralyzes their major muscles whenever they step into the kitchen is somehow held in check. Maybe that's because making breakfast is very much like working the outdoor barbecue—one pan, not a lot of ingredients, and a similar culinary approach—*la methode* "cook it 'til it's done."

At Dad's Diner feel free to offer the usual breakfast specials: Adam and Eve on a Raft, Whiskey down, and Slugs and Battery Acid. In addition here are some other tasty dishes the family might like as a change of pace. And who knows—your family may become regulars.

"Mornin' Pops," they'll say.

"What'll it be?" says you.

"The usual, Pops," they say, pulling up their chairs. "Gimme the usual."

MENU

Fruit and Yogurt Shakes
Stuffed French Toast
Cinnamon Crescents
Home Fries
Real Hot Chocolate

9

Fruit and Yogurt Shake

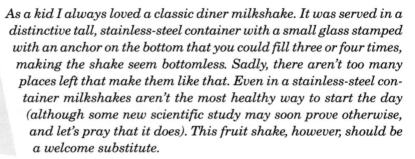

Note

You can substitute fresh or frozen blueberries for the strawberries.

If there's a restaurant supply store in your neck of the woods, you easily can pick up one of those stainless-steel shake containers to make the experience even more authentic.

Makes 4 servings

As a kid I always loved a classic diner milkshake. It was served in a distinctive tall, stainless-steel container with a small glass stamped with an anchor on the bottom that you could fill three or four times, making the shake seem bottomless. Sadly, there aren't too many places left that make them like that. Even in a stainless-steel container milkshakes aren't the most healthy way to start the day (although some new scientific study may soon prove otherwise, and let's pray that it does). This fruit shake, however, should be a welcome substitute.

2 cups fresh stemmed or frozen strawberries

1 ripe banana

1 cup orange juice

2 cups vanilla yogurt

Put all the ingredients in a blender and puree until smooth.

Stuffed French Toast

Makes 4 servings

French toast is one of those foods you can't really improve on, but you can add a little variation every once in a while. This version is made by sandwiching slices of ham and grated cheese between two pieces of bread, securing them with toothpicks, and then preparing them like regular French toast.

8 large eggs
¼ cup milk
8 slices white or whole wheat bread

¼ pound smoked ham—about 4 thin slices
¼ pound Cheddar cheese, grated
1 tablespoon butter

1. Beat the eggs together with the milk in a medium bowl.

2. Place 4 slices of the bread on the counter. Arrange a slice of the ham and 2 tablespoons of the grated cheese in the center of each slice. Place a second slice over the first and secure them together with toothpicks placed on an angle just inside the crust on all four sides. Repeat for the remaining three slices.

3. Place a large skillet over a medium heat. Add the butter to the pan and as it starts sizzling, spread it so that it evenly glazes the bottom. While the pan is heating, slip a spatula under one of the "sandwiches" and lower it into the eggs so that it is completely covered. Use the spatula to transfer it to the frying pan. Repeat with the remaining "sandwiches." Cook until the bottom of the sandwiches are golden brown, about 2 minutes, and then turn and cook 2 minutes more. Remove the toothpicks and serve immediately with real maple syrup.

Cinnamon Crescents

Makes 2 dozen

Dad's Diner is famous for this homemade pastry. Everyone who stops by has to have one with their coffee or hot chocolate. Customers think they take a long time to make, but when using his trusty food processor Dad knows that all he really has to do is shape the pastry into a circle, sprinkle on the filling, cut it into wedges, and roll them up. Dad should leave himself about an hour to put these together.

For the filling

1 cup chopped walnuts
½ cup sugar
1 tablespoon cinnamon
½ cup dried currants

For the pastry dough

1 cup less 1 tablespoon of lukewarm milk
1 package yeast
1 egg, beaten
3 cups flour
¼ cup sugar
1 cup (2 sticks) butter
4 ounces cream cheese
1 tablespoon water
1 egg, beaten, for brushing

Note

You can make the crescents in advance. For one day, store them at room temperature in a well-sealed plastic container. If you make them any more in advance than that, you should freeze them in a well-sealed plastic container. Take them out of the freezer the night before and let them thaw in the container at room temperature.

1. Mix all the ingredients for the filling together in a medium mixing bowl and set aside.

2. Measure the lukewarm milk into a medium mixing bowl and sprinkle on the yeast. Let it sit until the yeast has softened, about 4 minutes. Stir in the beaten egg.

3. Measure the flour and sugar into the bowl of a food processor. Add the butter and cream cheese and process in about 10 pulses until the butter is in small, pea-sized pieces.

4. With the processor on, quickly pour the milk mixture down the tube and continue processing until the dough forms into a ball. If it is too sticky, add more flour one tablespoon at a time. If it crumbles apart, add more milk one tablespoon at a time.

5. Divide the dough in half and shape it into two balls. Wrap one in wax paper and refrigerate while you work with the other.

6. Preheat the oven to 375°F and lightly butter a baking sheet. Sprinkle some flour on a clean counter and roll out the ball of dough into a circle about 10 inches across. Sprinkle half the filling mixture over the dough. Cut the circle into 12 wedges, like very thin slices of pie. Roll up each wedge, starting from the outer edge and rolling to the center so that it resembles a pastry crescent.

7. Place the crescent on the baking sheet and repeat with the remaining wedges. Leave about 2 inches between each pastry because they will expand when they are cooking.

8. Let the crescents rise at room temperature while you repeat steps 6 and 7 with the second ball of dough.

9. Lightly beat an egg in a small bowl with one tablespoon of water. Brush the tops of the crescents in the first pan and place them in the center rack of the oven. Bake for 15 to 17 minutes or until the tops are lightly browned. Remove the pan to a cooling rack. Brush the tops of the second pan of crescents and bake those.

Note

You really should have a food processor to make these. Otherwise they are too labor-intensive. If you are sans processor, you may consider the coffee cake on page 7 or buying some danish at a local bakery.

Home Fries

No self-respecting diner would be without these on the menu. Heck, I know some gourmands who are so home-fry obsessed that they order the breakfast special and tell the waitress to hold the eggs and toast.

1½ pounds new potatoes, washed
    and cut into quarters with their
    skins on

2 tablespoons vegetable oil

½ green bell pepper, diced

½ medium onion, diced

1 teaspoon garlic powder

1 teaspoon paprika

Salt and pepper

1. Immediately after cutting the potatoes into quarters, place them in a medium saucepan with enough cold water to cover them. Place the pan over high heat and bring the water to a boil. Reduce the heat to medium and allow the potatoes to simmer for 10 minutes. They should be not quite cooked through at this point. Drain the potatoes, shaking the strainer several times to get out as much water as possible.

2. Heat the oil in a large, heavy skillet over medium-high heat until it is hot, about 1 minute, making sure to spread the oil so it evenly glazes the bottom. Add the potatoes, pepper, and onion. Then cook, stirring often, for about 15 minutes or until the potatoes are cooked through and lightly brown. Sprinkle on the garlic powder, paprika, salt and pepper. Continue cooking until the potatoes take on a reddish color, about 3 minutes. Serve with ketchup and/or hot sauce.

Real Hot Chocolate

Makes 4 servings

Even at the counter at Dad's Diner, you don't want the young kids drinking coffee. There will be time enough for that by 6th grade (just kidding). But there's nothing wrong with a hot chocolate, which they can hunch over and sip just like coffee, pretending they're in an Edward Hopper painting.

3½ tablespoons cocoa powder
6 tablespoons sugar

¼ cup hot water
3 cups milk

1. Combine the cocoa and sugar into a medium saucepan. Add the hot water and use a whisk to stir the mixture into a thick paste. Add the milk in a slow, steady stream, stirring constantly as you do.

2. Place the pan over medium heat and continue to stir as the cocoa heats up. Continue heating and stirring until the cocoa is very warm. Do not let it boil.

3. Pour the cocoa through a strainer into 4 coffee cups and serve. If you don't see any lumps, pour it directly into the cups.

Fun and Games

Small-town diners wise to the tribulations of taking kids out to dinner supply a kid's menu with an accompanying activity sheet. Go to a local bookstore and buy some children's books with these game to keep the kids busy:

A. Maze

B. Dot to Dot

C. Stuff to color in

D. Hangman

E. Trivia questions to ask dad

    1. Who asked all the kids watching his TV show to go to their father's pants and "get out all that green stuff and send it to me?"

    2. What group sang the song *Incense and Peppermints*?

    3. What heavyweight boxing champ was stripped of his title and imprisoned for refusing to be drafted?

    4. What was the name of James West's sidekick in *Wild, Wild, West*?

    5. What TV show popularized the phrase "You bet your bippy?"

    6. What Broadway musical had the lyric "They'll be a ga-ga at the go-go/when they see me in my toga?"

Answers to trivia: 1. Soupy Sales   2. Strawberry Alarm Clock   3. Muhammed Ali   4. Artemis Gordon   5. *Laugh-In*   6. *Hair*

F. Diner talk lexicon

See if the kids can figure out what these examples of diner lingo actually mean.

Nickname	Dish
Slugs	Doughnuts
Through the garden	Lettuce and tomato
With wheels	To go
Adam and Eve on a raft	Eggs over easy with sausage links
Whiskey down	Rye toast
Draw one	Pour a cup of coffee
Battery acid	The coffee (also mud, java, joe)
86	All out of something
OJ up	Orange juice is ready
Wreck two	Two eggs scrambled

Cucina Fresca

Recipes make 8 servings

In Italy, you can truck down to your local deli (*salumeria*) and pick up the makings of a meal that would rival what you could get at many fancy Italian restaurants in New York. Not just the various prosciutto, salami, sopresata, and cheeses, but fabulous olives, roasted peppers, roasted squash, and fresh homemade salads, richly redolent of basil and garlic. A quick stop at the bakery—usually just a few doors away—for some breads, and you can painlessly put together a very respectable room-temperature meal for a fair-sized crowd.

Of course, we're not in Italy (corporeally, anyway) so we have to make do. If you live near Ann Arbor, Michigan, you can "make do" in glorious style by stopping at Zingerman's Deli. Ari Weinzweig, one of the proprietors, is unknowingly friend to hundreds of dads, who, when it's their turn to put a meal together, run down to Zingerman's to "get some stuff." Most cities usually have one source for Italian specialties. Seek it out. If you ask for something they don't stock, they may be able to order it for you.

MENU

Assorted Dried Sausages and Hams

Italian Cheeses

Olives

Plus the following homemade dishes:

Seafood Salad

Roasted Peppers

Bocancini

Caponata

Skillet Focaccia

Seafood Salad

The hint of lemon in the vinaigrette brings out the flavor of the shrimp, scallops, and squid. This recipe calls for medium shrimp, which are small enough so they only have to be shelled and not deveined. When buying the squid, see if you can get it already cleaned. You can make this dish up to 24 hours in advance. Store in a well-sealed plastic container in the refrigerator.

6 tablespoons olive oil

3 shallots, minced

4 cloves garlic, finely chopped

1 pound bay scallops

1 pound medium shrimp (36–40 size) cleaned

1 pound squid, cleaned and cut into ¼-inch rings

¼ cup extra-virgin olive oil

6 tablespoons freshly squeezed lemon juice

¼ cup fresh parsley, chopped

1½ teaspoon salt

Pinch of cayenne pepper

4 celery stalks, finely chopped

2 red bell peppers, diced

3 scallions, finely chopped

Note

If using cleaned, frozen shrimp, follow directions for thawing on the package.

1. Place a large frying pan on a high heat until it gets hot, about 2 minutes. Add 2 tablespoons of the olive oil and spread it so it glazes the bottom of the pan. Add half the shallots and garlic along with the scallops and cook, stirring frequently, until the scallops are opaque, 2 to 3 minutes. Transfer the scallops to the mixing bowl.

2. Return the pan to the heat, let it get hot, and add 2 tablespoons of olive oil. Add the shrimp and the remaining shallots and garlic and cook them, stirring frequently, until the shrimp are pink and opaque inside, 2 to 3 minutes. Transfer the shrimp to the mixing bowl.

3. Return the pan to the heat, let it get hot, and add 1 tablespoon of olive oil. Add half the squid and cook, stirring frequently until it is cooked through, about 3 minutes. Transfer the squid to the mixing bowl and cook the remaining squid in the same manner.

4. In a small mixing bowl, whisk together the extra-virgin olive oil and lemon juice, parsley, salt and cayenne. Add the celery, red pepper, and scallions to the seafood, pour the vinaigrette over it, and toss everything together gently. Refrigerate the salad until you're ready to serve it.

Roasted Peppers

Makes 8 servings as an appetizer

When friends come by and see a quartet of red and yellow peppers resting directly on the burners of my stove, they are apt to get alarmed. I quickly reassure them with some soothing words and a stiff drink that this is actually the best way to roast peppers indoors. If you don't have a gas range, however, you'll have to broil them in the oven. Besides the earthy flavor, the lush colors of the peppers enhance any table.

6 red bell peppers or a combination of red and yellow

Gas range method

1. Place the peppers directly on the burners and turn the flame on high. Use tongs to turn the peppers as they blacken on the bottom.

2. When the peppers are completely blackened, transfer them to a mixing bowl or brown paper shopping bag. Cover the bowl with a pan lid or aluminum foil or close the top of the paper bag and let the peppers sit for 20 minutes until they are cool. This procedure helps make the skin easier to peel off. Repeat with the remaining peppers.

3. Working over a clean bowl, use your hands to rub the charred black skin from the peppers. The bits of skin can be messy, so use a separate bowl as a repository for the cleaned peppers. If you can't get certain bits of black skin off the pepper, you can run it under cold water. But too much water diminishes the intensity of the flavor. When the peppers are clean, open them up and pull out the seeds and stem.

4. To serve, cut the peppers lengthwise into quarters and assemble them decoratively, alternating colors, on a platter.

Broiler method

1. Turn on the broiler. Place the peppers on a cookie sheet and broil 2 inches away from the heat, turning as the peppers blacken on top, about every 2 minutes.

2. Proceed as described in steps 2 through 4.

Music

You can't get more Italian than Verdi, and because this is a festive, less-than-formal party, selections from *La Traviata* or *Il Trovatore* might not overwhelm the evening. Equally Italian in sentiment and style is Nino Rota's film music, especially what he composed for Fellini. Put on some of Rota's music and your guests may have a visceral reaction as they flash back to a college date when they went to see *La Strada* or *La Dolce Vita*. At this point, the women should put on sunglasses and the men should remove their arms from the sleeves of their sport jackets and wear them slung over both shoulders. Oh, and everyone should drive home on their Vespas.

Bocancini

Makes 8 servings as an appetizer

Fresh mozzarella tastes great on its own, but adding a touch of olive oil and some red pepper gives it just a bit more zip.

½ cup olive oil
1 clove garlic, crushed
½ teaspoon red pepper flakes

1½ pounds mozzarella, preferably fresh
1 tablespoon fresh basil, chopped; or 1 teaspoon dried basil

1. Place the olive oil, garlic, and red pepper flakes in a small bowl and stir them together. Cover and let the mixture sit on the counter for at least 8 hours or overnight.

2. Cut the mozzarella into 1-inch pieces and put them in a mixing bowl. Remove the garlic clove and then pour the oil over the mozzarella. Toss well and serve.

Setting the Cucina Fresca Table

Literally "cool food," all the dishes in this meal are meant to be served at room temperature.

From the Deli
¾ pound thinly sliced prosciutto
¾ pound sweet sopresata
¾ pound hard salami
¾ pound sharp Italian cheese, such as aged provolone or an extra-sharp Cheddar
1 pound Italian black olives

Homemade
Boccancini
Roasted peppers
Caponata
Seafood salad
Focaccia

Store-Bought
Italian bread and/or semolina bread

Every visitor to Italy has a vivid memory of seeing their first antipasto table in the front of a restaurant. The rich colors and earthy aroma make a vivid impression. Here are a couple of tips to re-create that look:

- Put every dish in its own platter or bowl. Even the olives. It looks more opulent and highlights the food.

- Use platters or bowls that are of contrasting colors to the food. Use darker platters for lighter foods and vice versa.

Caponata

Spread on slices of Italian bread, this earthy appetizer will knock everyone's socks off. I once served it at a dinner party and everyone ate so much of it that they were almost too full for dinner. Next time, I made more caponata and no dinner at all. Caponata is one of those dishes in which the flavor intensifies if it sits for a day. If possible, make it the day before the party and refrigerate until ready to use.

½ cup yellow raisins

½ cup olive oil

1 medium eggplant, peeled and cut into ¾-inch rounds

1 large onion, peeled and cut into ½-inch slices

1 cup canned crushed tomatoes

1 teaspoon cocoa powder

16 Kalamata olives, pitted and coarsely chopped

¼ cup balsamic vinegar

1. Preheat the oven to 450°F. Fit one rack on the top third of the oven and one on the bottom third. While the oven is heating, cover the raisins in warm water and let them soak for 5 minutes. Then drain the water and set them aside.

2. Generously grease a baking pan with 2 tablespoons of the olive oil. Arrange the eggplant slices on the pan and brush the tops with 2 more tablespoons of olive oil. Bake the eggplant on the bottom rack until it is just cooked through, about 12 minutes. Turn on the broiler and cook the eggplant until it browns slightly, about 3 minutes. Remove the pan and let it cool on a rack.

3. Turn off the broiler and cook the onion slices in the same manner, baking them for 12 minutes, and then turning on the broiler and broiling them for 3 minutes or until they begin to brown. Let the onions cool as well. If your oven can accommodate two pans, you can bake the eggplant and onion at the same time. You still need to broil them separately, however.

4. In a large bowl, mix together the tomatoes, cocoa powder, chopped olives, and raisins. When the eggplant and onion have cooled, chop them coarsely and add them to the bowl. Pour on the balsamic vinegar and stir together. Season with salt and pepper to taste, cover, and refrigerate until ready to serve.

Skillet Focaccia

Makes one 10-inch loaf (8 servings)

Baking this Italian bread in a cast-iron skillet ensures the proper shape and a crispy crust. You'll need to start this early in the morning or make it the night before.

1⅓ **cups warm water**

1 **pinch sugar**

1 **package dry yeast**

⅓ **cup olive oil**

4 **cups unbleached, all-purpose flour**

1 **teaspoon salt**

1 **additional tablespoon olive oil**

1 **teaspoon dried rosemary**

1. Place the water in the bowl of a food processor fitted with a steel blade. Add the sugar and sprinkle on the yeast. Let the yeast stand until it foams, about 10 minutes.

2. Add first the olive oil then the flour and salt to the bowl and process until the mixture forms into a ball of smooth and elastic dough, about 30 seconds. Continue processing 1 minute more. If the dough is too dry and falls apart, add more warm water one tablespoon at a time. If the dough is too sticky, add more flour one tablespoon at a time.

Note

If you don't have a food processor, follow steps 1 and 2 using a mixing bowl instead of the processor bowl. Stir in the flour with a wooden spoon until it forms a ball of dough. You may have to use your hands for the last stages of this. Transfer the dough to a lightly floured board or counter and knead for 5 to 7 minutes, until the dough is smooth and elastic. (See page 86 for kneading tips.) Continue the recipe from step 3.

3. Transfer the dough to a lightly greased bowl, cover it with a dish towel, and let it rise in a warm, draft-free place until it doubles in size, about 2 hours.

4. When the dough has risen, punch it down, form it into a ball, and then flatten it into a 10-inch circle. Transfer the dough to a well-oiled, 10-inch, cast-iron skillet, cover with a towel, and let the dough rise until it doubles in size, about 1½ hours.

5. Preheat the oven to 400°F. When the dough has risen, brush the top with a little olive oil, sprinkle with salt and the rosemary leaves, and bake on the center rack of the oven for 20 minutes or until the top is light brown. Let the focaccia cool for 20 minutes before removing it from the skillet.

The Five Most Asked Questions About Olive Oil

1. What does "extra-virgin" mean?

Extra-virgin olive oil, or as they say in Italian, *extra-virgine*, is made from the first pressing of the olives and has the most flavor. It's like the difference between the richness of the coffee when it first runs through the grounds versus the coffee that comes through at the end.

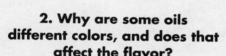

2. Why are some oils different colors, and does that affect the flavor?

The different colors of the oil are a result of the different colors of the olives. Though it may seem like the darker oils have a more robust flavor, there is no actual correlation between color and flavor.

3. If I pay more, do I really get a better oil?

Yes and no. Like wines, there are olive oils in the midprice range that are quite satisfactory and will most certainly enhance the flavor of the foods with which you use them. But the best oils are expensive. Be sure to do some research before paying a lot of money, however, because you could wind up with a fancy bottle of oil that has little to distinguish it from the one you use every day. Extra-virgin oils by producers such as Colonna, Agrumato, Nunñez de Prado, Moulin Jean, or Tenuta de Numerouno are well worth the money.

4. Do I need to use extra-virgin oil when I'm cooking, like when I make my tomato sauce?

The debate about whether it makes a difference sautéing foods in extra-virgin oil still continues. Some say the subtlety of the flavor is lost once it comes into contact with high heat. Others say they can tell the difference. I think it's not worth using your best oil for cooking. Use regular olive oil or a less expensive extra-virgin for cooking and save the more expensive stuff for salads, pasta, and other dishes where you can appreciate it's flavor.

5. What's the best thing I can do with a really fine olive oil?

Put about ½ cup in a small bowl with a mashed clove of garlic, let it sit for an hour, and then dip some great Italian bread into it while you're sipping a hearty Chianti.

drinks

Wine Selections

If it's not obvious that an Italian wine is in order here, then you haven't been paying enough attention. Look for one of these wines or ask for a similar one from the region.

Red

From Sicily:
Cosimo Taurino or Corvo
Chianti from Tuscany:
Such as Antinori
Dolcetto from Piedmont:
Such as Also Conterno

White

Pino Bianco from Friuly

Negroni

Makes 1 Cocktail

A great cocktail to start off the evening. The slight tartness of the Compari is balanced by the sweetness of the Vermouth while the vodka gives it a little kick.

2 ounces (4 tablespoons) vodka

1 ounce (2 tablespoons) Compari

1 ounce (2 tablespoons) sweet vermouth

Thin slice of orange

1. Pour the liquors into a cocktail glass with ice.

2. Stir well and garnish with a slice of orange.

Grappa

Grappa is a kind of Italian brandy traditionally made from what's usually discarded after wine making, namely the skins and pits of the grapes. Grappa has developed a reputation as being harsh and irascible, the Lee Marvin of liquor. This is due to the fact that only the least-expensive and poorest-produced grappas were available. Now that grappa has become chic in Italy, the after-dinner drink of choice among the paparazzi, some of the smaller producers who make softer, more refined grappa are now being imported. You should be able to find some at a well-stocked wine shop. Then you can end your meal just as you would if you were hosting your party in Florence and sending your guests off to their homes across the Arno.

Champagne and Dessert

Recipes make 12 servings

The invitation reads "Please join us for champagne and dessert." That's all you need to say, and good karma will emanate from the card. Dessert parties always work, but they work especially well if you have a backyard or large patio. You can string up some Chinese lanterns, set up a few white-clothed cocktail tables with votive candles, and light some citronella torches to discourage the bugs. Then all that's left is to have a few square yards of dance floor in case anyone feels like a fox-trot or the hully gully once the champagne kicks in. It's also a plus to have a little boathouse by the water, the locale of choice for an illicit tryst.

Call the party for nine o'clock. Friday or Saturday nights are best. Guests will eat dinner before they arrive. With the money you've saved by not serving a main course, spring for some fabulous champagne.

MENU

Lightened Grand Marniér Cheese Pie
Almost Flourless Chocolate Cake
Thumbprint Cookies
Fresh Fruit Platter
Lemon Poppy Seed Cake
Coffee and Tea
Champagne

Note

The cheese pies will keep well overnight, but don't wrap them in plastic, or the crusts will get soggy and the filling will lose its proper consistency. Try to get some pie boxes from a local bakery and refrigerate the pies in the boxes.

Lightened Grand Marniér Cheese Pie

Makes two pies (16 to 20 servings)

This variation on the classic cheese cake takes advantage of the low-fat and non-fat cream cheese now available. The consistency and flavor are hardly distinguishable from the original, which is a vortex of cholesterol and fat. Preparing most of this in the blender and using ready-made graham-cracker crusts makes this the simplest of the desserts on the menu to prepare.

12 ounces "light" cream cheese or Nuftachel

12 ounces nonfat cream cheese

½ cup sugar

2 tablespoons Grand Marniér or other orange-flavored liquor

2 tablespoons skim milk

2 teaspoons grated orange peel

1 teaspoon vanilla extract

3 egg yolks

6 egg whites

2 premade graham cracker pie crusts

You might want to throw this party after the opening of a play. In this case, one of the activities can be reading the reviews when they first hit the newsstands.
The problem is that a bad review can ruin the party. It might be best to get the papers yourself, check the spirit of the notice, and then either bring them in triumphantly or throw them in the trash and claim the deliveryperson went out on strike.

1. Preheat the oven to 350°F.

2. Place all the ingredients except the egg whites and pie crusts in a blender or food processor and blend together until very smooth. Transfer the mixture to a large mixing bowl.

3. In a separate bowl, beat the egg whites with a hand mixer until they form stiff peaks, about 1½ minutes. Using a large rubber spatula, fold the egg whites gently into the cream cheese mixture.

4. Pour the mixture into the two pie crusts and bake on the center rack of the oven until the pies are set in the middle, about 25 minutes. Let them cool for an hour before refrigerating.

Almost Flourless Chocolate Cake

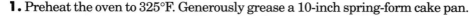

Makes one 10-inch cake (16 to 20 servings)

1 pound bittersweet or semisweet chocolate, broken into pieces	**2 cups sugar**
1¾ cups (3 sticks) butter	**1 cup all-purpose, unbleached flour**
12 eggs, separated	**¼ cup cocoa**

1. Preheat the oven to 325°F. Generously grease a 10-inch spring-form cake pan.

2. Melt the chocolate and butter on the top of a double boiler, stirring occasionally. When it is completely melted, remove it from the heat and let it cool slightly.

3. In a large mixing bowl, cream the egg yolks and sugar with an electric mixer on medium speed until the mixture is smooth and pale yellow, about 3 minutes.

4. Add the cooled chocolate mixture to the egg yolks and sugar and beat together with the electric mixer until it is completely incorporated, about 2 minutes. Add the flour and cocoa and continue mixing until they are completely incorporated.

5. In a separate bowl, beat the egg whites until they form stiff peaks. Do not overbeat. Be sure to fully clean the beaters before using them on the egg whites.

6. Stir ⅓ of the egg whites into the batter with a large rubber spatula. Gently fold in the remaining egg whites.

7. Transfer the batter to the cake pan and bake on the center rack of the oven for about 1 hour and 15 minutes or until a toothpick inserted into the center comes out with little flecks of cake (not smeared cake).

8. Let the cake cool for 1 hour on a cooling rack before removing the cake pan. Let the cake cool another hour before serving.

Note

If you don't have a double boiler, you can use a medium stainless-steel bowl placed on top of a medium saucepan half-full of water.

You can make this cake up to two weeks before the party and store it in the freezer. Let it cool completely (about 4 hours) before wrapping it in one layer of plastic wrap and one layer of aluminum foil. Be sure to allow 6 hours for the cake to thaw at room temperature. Remove the plastic wrap while it is thawing to avoid condensation, which can make the top of the cake soggy.

Thumbprint Cookies

Makes 4 dozen cookies

These demure little cookies are just right to nibble with champagne. Have the kids help you make the dents on top for the jam.

1 cup walnuts

1 cup (2 sticks) butter at room temperature

½ cup brown sugar

2 egg yolks, separated

1 teaspoon vanilla

1 cup unbleached, all-purpose flour

8 ounces strawberry jam

Music

Recordings by Frank Sinatra, Judy Garland, and Fats Waller are a must for this party—swinging without being too overwhelming. Also appropriate is the sultry album *John Coltrane and Johnny Hartman*. Although I could see at certain points if you wanted something more poppish—some Lovin' Spoonful, early Beatles, some Bob Wills and his Texas Playboys, or the best of Buffalo Springfield. Toward the end of the party, you might want to spin some platters of Nat King Cole ballads, in case anyone's in the mood for slow dancing.

1. Preheat the oven to 375°F. Place the walnuts in the bowl of a food processor fitted with a metal blade. Pulse until they are ground into tiny pieces the size of split peas, about 6 to 8 pulses. If you don't have a processor, you'll need to spend the several minutes it will take to chop the nuts very finely by hand. Transfer to a small mixing bowl and set aside.

2. In a medium mixing bowl, cream together the butter and sugar with a wooden spoon until they are well combined, about 2 minutes. Add the egg yolks and vanilla and mix well. Add the flour and stir until it is completely incorporated. Beat the egg whites gently with a fork for one minute to lighten them, and then set them aside.

3. Roll the dough into 1-inch balls. Dip the balls lightly into the egg white and then roll them in the chopped walnuts. Place them on an ungreased cookie sheet 1 inch apart. Bake the cookies on the center rack for 5 minutes.

4. Remove the pan and press your thumb into the center of each cookie, making a dent about halfway down. Fill the dent with slightly less than one teaspoon of jam. When all the cookies are filled, return them to the oven for 8 more minutes or until the bottoms are lightly brown. Remove the pan and let it cool for 30 minutes on a cooling rack before removing the cookies from the pan.

Lemon Poppy Seed cake

Makes 12 to 16 servings

This is the one dessert you really need to make the day of the party. You'll also need a 9½-inch tube pan. Any decent kitchen supply store will have one. Just tell the person behind the counter what you need and why. He or she will be suitably impressed.

1½ cups unbleached, all-purpose flour

2 teaspoons baking powder

1 cup (2 sticks) butter at room temperature

1⅓ cups sugar

1 cup sour cream

3 eggs

¼ cup poppy seeds

3 tablespoons fresh lemon juice

1 tablespoon fresh lemon rind

For the topping

1 tablespoon fresh lemon juice

½ cup confectioner's sugar

1. Preheat the oven to 350°F. Generously grease a 9½-inch tube pan with butter and lightly dust it with flour. In a medium mixing bowl, stir together the flour and baking soda with a whisk until they are well combined.

2. In a medium mixing bowl, cream together the sugar and butter with a wooden spoon until the mixture is well blended, about 3 minutes. Add the sour cream and stir until it is blended in. Add the eggs one at a time, stirring until each is incorporated. Add the poppy seeds, lemon juice, and lemon rind and stir well. Add the flour mixture and stir until it is just incorporated.

3. Use a rubber spatula to transfer the batter to the tube pan, making sure that it is distributed evenly. Bake on the center rack for 50 to 55 minutes or until a toothpick inserted in the center comes out clean. Let the cake cool for 20 minutes and then remove it from the pan in one swift motion. Turn over the pan and bang it down onto a clean counter. Lift the pan away and use a spatula to carefully transfer the cake to a serving tray.

4. For the topping, in a medium bowl, combine the lemon juice and confectioner's sugar with a fork. When it is well blended, drizzle it over the top of the cake. Place the cake in a plastic cake storer until it is ready to serve. If you don't have a cake storer, wrap the cake in plastic when it is unfrosted, and drizzle on the glaze just before serving.

Fresh Fruit Platter

Makes 12 servings

A colorful assortment of fruits enhances the dessert table. It also gives some of the guests watching their weight something to eat for seconds.

1 ripe honeydew or cranshaw melon, or a large cantaloupe

1 ripe pineapple

1 pound seedless red grapes, rinsed and cut into small bunches

1 pound seedless green grapes, rinsed and cut into small bunches

2 pints ripe strawberries, stemmed

1. Cut the melon in half lengthwise and scoop out the seeds. Again slice the melon lengthwise into 1½-inch wedges. Use a paring knife to slice the flesh from the rind. With the melon flesh still resting in place on the rind, cut it into 2-inch pieces. Put a toothpick through each piece, deep enough so that the point secures into the rind.

2. Cut the top off the pineapple and save it. Cut the pineapple in half lengthwise, and then lengthwise again into 1½-inch wedges. Trim the triangular strip of core from each wedge. Continue as in step 1 for the melon, slicing the flesh from the rind. Then, with the pineapple meat resting in place on the rind, cut it into 1-inch pieces. Put a toothpick through each piece, deep enough so the point secures into the rind.

3. Place the pineapple top in the center of a large platter. Arrange the melon and pineapple in alternating sections like spokes on a wheel. Arrange the grapes in clusters between the melon and pineapple sections. Scatter the strawberries around the platter. Cover the fruit with lightly damp paper towels and store in the refrigerator until you're ready to serve it.

Coffee

A cup of coffee is a nice way to cap off the evening. It's also a service to your guests who have to drive home, giving them a few moments to gather their wits and a little boost to perk them up. Make one pot of decaf and one of regular.

A Champagne Primer

Lots of sparkling wines are called champagne, but as you probably know, only bubbly made from grapes grown in the Champagne region of France can be classified as true champagne. And if you ever tasted real champagne, served properly, you know that it's all good. That's right, and you can quote me, there is no such thing as bad champagne.

Serving

Champagne needs to be served very cold. The refrigerator will get it started, but to get the bottles sufficiently cold you really need to keep them on ice. This means not simply resting the bottle on ice but *surrounding* it to get it properly chilled. If you're serving champagne, you really should use appropriate champagne glasses—preferably, the tall, thin flutes. (Although if any of the guests, either men or women, are Tallulah Bankhead wannabes, sporting elbow-length black gloves, holding foot-long cigarette holders, and prone to expressions like "Daaaah-ling, you are just too, too tehhh-ribly funny," make sure that you have a few of the classic wide, flat champagne glasses on hand.)

Amounts

You should get 7 to 8 servings from each bottle if you fill the glasses ¾ full. But because people tend to drink more champagne than they should, figure on four bottles, plus one extra, just in case, and one more to have left over in the fridge.

Which to Buy

What champagne you get depends entirely on your budget. Five bottles of true champagne will set you back at least a C-note. See whether your favorite wine merchant has anything on sale. You might want to get a couple of different kinds and do a little tasting. If so, don't save the best for last. After two glasses, most of your guests won't be able to tell Cristal from a very dry ginger ale.

Some less expensive real champagnes (around $21 a bottle)

Perrier Jouet Brut

Moet and Chandon Imperial

Moet and Chandon White Star

Charles Heidsieck Brut

Roederer Brut

Tattinger Brut

Veuve Clicquot Brut

Some expensive real champagnes (between $50 and $120 a bottle)

Bollinger '88

Krug

Veuve Clicquot "Le Grande Dame"

Cuvee Dom Perignon

Roederer Cristal

For a list of more economical sparkling wines, see page 3.

Seductive Dinner for Two

Recipes make 2 servings

Since the birth of civilization, philosophers, poets, and lovers have held to the belief that certain foods had the ability to induce and heighten sensuality. This particular meal combines many of the foods considered to be the most potent aphrodisiacs—oysters, olives, lamb, and chocolate. All you need is a compelling reason to make it and a quiet place to go after dessert.

It's Mother's Day, and you want to give your wife a special treat. Or maybe it's Father's Day and you want your wife to give *you* a special treat. Perhaps the kids are staying at your parents' house for the night and the two of you have the place to yourselves. Or if you're a single dad, you could actually be dating again, and this dinner is the centerpiece of your amorous plans. Whatever the scenario, this is a menu that's designed for seduction. The dishes are sensuous and luscious. The ingredients were chosen for their amorous potency, designed to get someone in the mood, or if they're already in the mood, to keep them in it longer.

In anticipation of your evening's adventure, you'll need to prepare the venue. You want the table set just right, soft music on the hi-fi, the appropriate wine, and if it's a first date, all incriminating artifacts removed from your medicine cabinet.

MENU

Crostini with Goat Cheese and Pumpkin Seeds

Fresh Linguini with Oysters, Tomato, Saffron, and Cream

Sauteed Loin Lamb Chops with Dried Cherry Sauce

Warm Fudge Browine with Chocolate Ice Cream

Aphrodisiacs—Pro and More Pro

Food and sex are inexorably linked. They are both sensual and indulgent, using all the senses and most of the same organs, and are wonderful experiences to share with someone else.

Although it has never been scientifically proven, many foods have historically been endowed with aphrodisiac potency—among them oysters, turtle, lobster, shrimp, steak tartare, caviar, shark fin soup, garlic, clams, muscles, and chocolate. Vegetables of a certain shape that would make Priapus proud have also been thought to enhance the prodigiousness of the member of the consuming male. Unfortunately, the most highly celebrated aphrodisiac, bull's balls, which, thinly sliced and sautéed, induce great desire in the female and immense prowess in the male, are unlikely to pop up at your local meat counter. But if you find some, by all means serve them up. The common euphemistic name for this dish is *Mountain Oysters*.

That said, on to the meal.

Crostini with Goat Cheese and Pumpkin Seeds

Makes approximately 20 crostini

Anything having to do with a goat, one of the most notoriously randy creatures on God's green earth, will help get the evening off to a rousing start.

1 thin loaf French or Italian bread,
   cut into ¾-inch slices
½ cup extra-virgin olive oil
Salt

4 ounces goat cheese
1 ounce pumpkin seeds

1. Preheat the oven to 350°F. Pour the olive oil into a small bowl. Dip both sides of a slice of bread into the olive oil so they are very lightly coated. Don't worry if a little bit of the bread is left dry. Place the slice on a baking sheet and repeat with the rest of the slices, arranging them in a single layer on the pan. Bake for 18 minutes or until the crostini is slightly brown. Transfer to a platter to cool.

2. Reduce the oven to 300°F. Spread 12 crostini with goat cheese. Store the rest in a plastic bag for a later date. Arrange 3 or 4 pumpkin seeds on the cheese, and then place them on a baking sheet. Heat them in the oven until they are warmed through, 3 to 5 minutes. Serve immediately.

Fresh Linguini with Oysters, Tomato, Saffron, and Cream

Makes 2 servings

Casanova is reputed to have eaten four dozen oysters for dinner on a regular basis to help fuel his lust. While I cannot personally attest to the merits of eating so many, I did have six oysters one evening before a tryst and in the course of a long, joyous night, three of the six definitely worked. Garlic's properties of inducing desire have been heralded by Homer, Aristotle, Rabelais, and other lovers and chefs throughout history. Oriental chroniclers of the sensual and erotic speak rapturously of the onion and shallot's ability to heighten sexual achievement. Tomatoes, or "scarlet love apples," have a rapacious reputation, perhaps because of their shape or texture. And who can forget Marty, that icon of fifties loneliness, his mother imploring him to go to the Waverly Ballroom to meet a couple of "nice tomatoes." Saffron too, has a long history of amorous mystique, having been used by the Phoenicians centuries ago to flavor the moon-shaped love cakes they offered to their fertility goddess. And as for butter and cream, well, a few tablespoons in the right context never hurt anyone.

¼ cup warm water

½ teaspoon saffron threads

4 ripe plum tomatoes, cut lengthwise into quarters

1 tablespoon sweet butter

2 shallots, finely chopped

1 clove garlic, finely chopped

12 oysters, shucked

¼ white wine

¼ cup heavy cream

Chopped fresh parsley

1. Measure the warm water into a small bowl and let the saffron soak until it is needed.

2. Use a small knife to trim away the seeds and inner membrane of the tomatoes, and then slice each tomato quarter lengthwise into thirds.

3. Place a medium skillet over medium-high heat. Add the butter to the pan and as it starts sizzling, spread it so that it evenly glazes the bottom. Add the shallots and cook until they are soft, stirring frequently, about 2 minutes. Add the garlic and cook 1 minute more.

4. Add the oysters to the pan, reserving any liquid, and cook, stirring frequently, until the oysters are cooked through, about 2 minutes.

5. Add the wine and cook until reduced by half. Then add the cream and the saffron with its water and any oyster liquid and stir well so that the saffron is fully incorporated into the sauce. Add salt to taste. Cook the sauce until it is heated through, about 2 minutes. Spoon the sauce over the cooked pasta, making sure that the oysters are evenly dispersed, although you might want to give your guest a few extra.

Note

Because fresh pasta only takes 2 to 3 minutes to cook, you can begin cooking the pasta as soon as the sauce is done. Just make sure you allow enough time for the water to come to a boil before the sauce is done. If you can find squid ink pasta, it makes for a more dramatic presentation, with the red tomatoes and brilliant yellow of the sauce set off against the black pasta. And besides, the Romans had great faith in the ability of squid and octopus to keep a man young and vibrant.

What happens while you're in the kitchen?

With all the ingredients properly prepared and the water boiling, it should take you about 8 minutes to assemble the pasta and sauce. Your guest will need something to do. If it's your wife, or someone else familiar with the details of your domain, this would be a nice time to present them with a gift—something to look at, to clasp around her neck, to slip into later. If it is someone new to your house, it could be a good time to let them surreptitiously discover something wonderful about you. A shelf full of Oscars or a wall of platinum albums, perhaps, or your latest novel, strategically placed on the coffee table. Not everyone, however, has such rich achievements to display. You can try leaving your balance sheets for the last quarter with circles around the figures showing that profits are up, but I wouldn't recommend it. Likewise, little league trophies or copies of your high school graduation speech won't make a very sterling impression. You might have to settle for letting her wander about and, hopefully, begin developing a fondness for you. Just make sure there are no old socks or underwear lying around. But having a copy of an Anne Tyler, Lee Smith, or Barbara Kingsolver novel resting casually by your bed isn't a bad idea. It shows you're a sensitive, literate kind of guy. And you might even enjoy reading them.

Sautéed Loin Lamb Chops with Dried Cherry Sauce

Makes 2 servings

Of all meats, lamb is the one considered to be the greatest aphrodisiac. Think about Mary's little lamb, and why he was following her around all day. In the early part of this century, a doctor by the name of Paul Neihans had quite a reputation in Europe for increasing sexual longevity and potency by injecting the cells from the crushed organs of newborn lambs into some very famous people, such as Gloria Swanson, Noel Coward, and Thomas Mann. Turkish chefs created a provocatively shaped lamb croquette they called "Lady's Thigh." Coupled with the cherry sauce, this dish should continue the amorous course the meal already has taken.

To make the cherry sauce
¹/₂ cup (2 ounces) dried cherries
¹/₂ cup boiling water
1 tablespoon butter
2 shallots, finely chopped

¹/₄ cup port or sherry
³/₄ cup water
1 chicken bouillon cube

Note

The cherry sauce can be made the day before. Refrigerate it in a well-sealed plastic container. You might need to thin it out with a tablespoon of water when reheating.

1. Put the cherries in a small bowl and cover with the boiling water. Let them soak for 5 minutes.

2. Place a medium skillet over medium-high heat. Add the butter to the pan and as it starts sizzling, spread it so that it evenly glazes the bottom. Add the shallots and cook, stirring frequently, until they are soft, about 2 minutes.

3. Add the port or sherry to the pan and cook, stirring continuously, until it is reduced by half, about 1 minute.

4. Add the cherries, water, bouillon cube, and ¹/₂ cup of the cherry soaking liquid to the pan and stir until the bouillon cube is dissolved. Transfer the sauce to a blender and puree until it is just smooth. Thin with additional tablespoons of cherry liquid if the sauce is too thick to pour. Pour the sauce into a small pan to reheat while you are cooking the chops.

For the lamb chops
Salt and pepper
4 loin lamb chops
1 tablespoon olive oil

1 tablespoon butter
Chopped fresh parsley for garnish
$1/4$ cup port or sherry

1. Lightly salt and pepper the lamb chops and let them come to room temperature before cooking. This usually takes about 20 minutes.

2. Place a large skillet on a high heat. Add the oil in a small pool in the center of the pan. Place the butter in the oil. As soon as the butter starts sizzling, spread it so that it evenly glazes the bottom.

3. Place the chops in the pan and cook until they are a nice brown on the bottom, about 5 minutes. Turn and cook them 5 minutes more.

4. Transfer the chops to a platter and pour out any fat from the pan. Quickly return the pan to the heat and add $1/2$ cup of port or sherry. Use a spatula to scrape up any bits of lamb stuck to the bottom of the pan and then pour the liquid into the cherry sauce.

5. Spoon a pool of sauce onto the center of each dinner plate so that it covers all but a 1-inch rim around the outside. Place the chops in the pool of sauce. Garnish with a sprig of fresh parsley.

What to Do While You're Cooking the Lamb

Invite her into the kitchen. You've got one thing to do here—cook the lamb, which involves simply heating the pan, putting in the chops, and turning them over. Because it's so easy, try to look good doing it. Instead of worrying about the food, work on your attitude, your savvy use of the tongs, the casual way you take a sip of wine while the chops sizzle. I can assure you there will never be any scientific evidence that specific foods seduce women on their own, but I can say firsthand that cooking for a woman is the true aphrodisiac. Forget Spanish fly. Two perfectly cooked chops with a succulent sauce that she saw you cook *just for her* will give you your strongest chance at connubial bliss.

Warm Fudge Brownie with Chocolate Ice Cream

Makes 2 servings (with extra brownies left over)

It's a Haiku. It's an epiphany.

Lovers holding hands in soft moonlight
Ice cream on a warm fudge brownie.

Ezra Pound would have been proud.

4 ounces bittersweet or semisweet chocolate

1/2 cup (1 stick) butter

2/3 cup all-purpose, unbleached flour

1/4 cup cocoa powder

1/2 teaspoon baking powder

2 large eggs

1/2 cup sugar

1 teaspoon vanilla extract

1. Preheat the oven to 350°F. Grease an 8x8-inch baking pan and lightly dust it with flour.

2. Melt the chocolate and butter on top of a double boiler, stirring occasionally until the mixture is combined. While the chocolate is melting, mix the flour, cocoa powder, and baking powder with a whisk until it is combined. When the chocolate is melted, remove it from the heat.

3. In a medium mixing bowl, cream together the eggs and sugar with an electric mixer on medium speed until the mixture is smooth and pale yellow, about 3 minutes. Add the vanilla and chocolate mixture and continue to mix on medium speed until well combined. Add the flour mixture to the batter and mix until it is just incorporated.

4. Transfer the batter to the prepared pan and bake on the center rack for 22 minutes or until the center is set and a toothpick inserted in the center comes out not smeared but with little chocolate flecks attached. Let the brownies cool on a rack for 1 hour before cutting them into squares.

Note

You can make the brownies the day before you serve them. Let them cool completely, cut them into 2-inch squares, and store them in a well-sealed plastic container with wax paper between layers. Wrapped the same way, they can also be made up to one month in advance and frozen. Let the brownies defrost overnight at room temperature.

5. To serve, heat the brownies in a 300°F oven or the microwave for a few seconds until they are warm. Place each brownie on a plate and accompany it with a scoop of chocolate or vanilla ice cream.

Music

Music is very crucial to an evening of romance. It should compliment the various stages of the evening. In the fifties, a man had Mood Music—overly arranged albums with a sultry dame on the cover, showing lots of *décolletage* and a certain willingness, as if all she needed was the lush sound of 1,001 Strings to send her sliding supine onto the couch.

Mood albums and other recordings that fall under the heading "Space Age Bachelor Pad Music" are now being reissued.
Also, here are other appropriate choices:

Stage 1: Cocktails and Appetizers

West Coast cool would be in order—Chet Baker or Paul Desmond. Pianists Errol Garner or Tommy Flanagan would also have the right touch. If it's pop, maybe Joni Mitchell or Van Morrison, although that might provoke a Music Discussion—a potentially volatile undertaking you may not want to get involved in.

Stage 2: Dinner

Here the music needs to be sumptuous without being schmaltzy. Jazz choices might be Johnny Hodges, Bill Evans, or the album *Coltrane/Ballads*. Classical selections include a Debussy string quartet, some Ravel Trios, or the always suggestive piano music of Satie. Stay away from pop, although a little Brazilian music might be nice—early Caetano Veloso or Gilberto Gil providing a sensuous Bahian groove.

Stage 3: Post-Prandial Bliss

Something very sultry here. Ben Webster playing ballads is unequivocally recommended, a proven accompaniment to sensual pleasures. Also Frank Sinatra's, *In the Wee Small Hours*; Ella Fitzgerald's *The Intimate Ella*; or anything by Little Jimmy Scott.

Do-Ahead Dinner for Eight

Recipes make 8 servings

The beauty of this meal is that it's all cooked ahead of time, so all you have to do is reheat it right before the party. You'll need to spend some time on the preparations, although by no means do you have to do it all in one day. The veal can be cooked up to a few weeks in advance and frozen. The arugala can be washed and the dressing assembled the night before. And the icebox cake actually requires a day of rest in the refrigerator, though you'll have to steel yourself against cutting off a slice before dinner. By employing these and some other simple strategies, you can put the meal together without too much effort.

But that doesn't mean Dad still can't get a lot of mileage out of the time spent preparing this dinner. I see your being able to put off cleaning the garage for several weeks, claiming that you're working on one aspect of this meal or another. Likewise, any raking, spackling, straightening of the basement, or taking down the storm windows will need to be deferred until all preparations for the meal are complete.

Because all the food is prepared in advance, you can spend a good part of the afternoon relaxing. Feel free to read some Zen poetry, to practice your fly casting, or to think up a rhyme for *Aurora Borealis* in the lyrics to the song you're writing until minutes before the guests arrive. Just remember to leave time for a shower.

MENU

Shrimp and Fennel with
Citrus Vinaigrette
Arugula Salad with Shaved Parmesan
Veal and Wild Mushroom Stew
Icebox Cake

Shrimp and Fennel with Citrus Vinaigrette

Makes 8 servings as an appetizer

This is a simple yet delectable way to serve shrimp. I sometimes feel a little guilty pulling this dish out of the fridge ready-made just before the guests arrive. It almost seems too easy, but it doesn't stop me.

2 pounds large shrimp, peeled
   and deveined

1 red pepper, cored, seeded, and
   diced

1 yellow pepper, cored, seeded,
   and diced

1 medium fennel bulb, diced

½ medium red onion, diced

¼ cup orange juice, preferably
   freshly squeezed

¼ cup balsamic vinegar

1 teaspoon salt

Several dashes Tabasco sauce

Note

The salad can sit in the refrigerator for up to 4 hours.

1. Bring 4 quarts of water to a boil in a large pot. Add the shrimp and cook them until they are just cooked through, pink on the outside and opaque in the middle, about 3 minutes.

2. Drain the shrimp and rinse them in cold water until they cool down, about 2 minutes. Drain the shrimp well and pat them dry with a paper towel. Transfer the shrimp to a medium bowl and add the rest of the ingredients. Mix everything together, cover the bowl with plastic wrap, and refrigerate for at least 1 hour. Serve chilled on a bed of lettuce or radicchio.

Arugula Salad with Shaved Parmesan

Makes 8 servings

Because this is a hearty meal, this simple salad is all you'll need to serve before dessert.

3 large bunches arugala
¼ cup fresh lemon juice
¼ cup extra-virgin olive oil
½ teaspoon salt

One 4-ounce piece Parmesan cheese, preferably Parmigiano-Reggiano
Fresh pepper

1. Wash and dry the arugala. In a medium bowl, whisk together the lemon juice and salt. Continue to whisk as you slowly add the olive oil.

2. Arrange the arugala on individual salad plates. Use a vegetable peeler to shave off a few strips of Parmesan and drape them over the arugala. Drizzle a tablespoon of the dressing over each salad along with some freshly ground pepper.

Note

You can wash and dry the arugala the night before serving it. Store in a well-sealed plastic bag along with a few sheets of paper towel. You can make the dressing one day in advance. Store in a well-sealed jar or plastic container in the refrigerator.

Veal and Wild Mushroom Stew

Makes 8 servings

This is an earthy, succulent stew that will warm your cockles on a blustery fall evening. The most troublesome part of the recipe is allowing time for the porcini mushrooms to soak and then straining the soaking liquid. The rest of the dish goes together rather easily after that.

2 cups warm water

6 ounces dried porcini mushrooms

8 tablespoons olive oil

4 pounds boneless veal shoulder, cut into 1½-inch pieces

1 cup red wine

3 onions, thinly sliced

2 pounds portobello mushrooms, cut into ½-inch slices

5 cloves garlic, coarsely chopped

2 cups water

2 chicken bouillon cubes

8 ounces peeled baby carrots

1 pound new potatoes, cut in half

Salt and pepper

1. Place 2 cups of warm water into a medium mixing bowl. Add the dried porcini and let them soak for 4 hours at room temperature until they are soft. When they have soaked sufficiently, remove them from the liquid and place them in a strainer. *Do not throw away the soaking liquid because it will be used in the stew.* Rinse the mushrooms gently, looking for any bits of dirt. When they are rinsed, set them aside. Line a small strainer with a paper towel or piece of cheese cloth. Pour the porcini soaking liquid through to remove any dirt. Set the strained liquid aside.

2. Preheat the oven to 325°F. Place a large frying pan over high heat and let it get very hot, about 2 minutes. Add 2 tablespoons of the oil and one pound of the veal pieces. Cook until they are nicely brown on the bottom, about 4 minutes. Then turn them with your tongs and brown the other side. Transfer the browned veal to a 12x17-inch casserole dish. Return the pan to the heat and continue to brown the remaining veal one pound at a time. Add 1 tablespoon of oil to the pan and let the pan get hot before each batch of veal.

Note

You can make the stew up to two days in advance. The flavor will only get more intense as it sits covered in the refrigerator. Allow the stew to cool before storing in a well-sealed plastic container. You also can freeze the stew up to three weeks in advance. Let the stew partially thaw in the refrigerator overnight. Reheat in a large pot on the stove over medium heat.

3. When all the meat is browned, add the red wine and scrape the bottom of the pan to release all the little pieces of meat that have stuck to it. Transfer the liquid to the casserole.

4. Wipe out the pan, place it over medium-high heat, and let it get hot, about 1 minute. Add 3 more tablespoons of the oil and spread it so it evenly glazes the bottom. Add the onion slices and portobello mushrooms and cook, stirring frequently, until the onions are soft, about 6 minutes. Add the porcini mushrooms and cook, stirring frequently, 3 minutes more. Then add the garlic and cook 1 minute more, stirring continuously. Transfer the onion/mushroom mixture to the casserole. Add two cups of water to the pan along with the bouillon cubes and stir until they are dissolved. Transfer the liquid to the casserole.

5. Add the carrots and potatoes to the casserole along with liquid from the porcini mushrooms and cover the pan. Place the casserole on the center rack of the oven and cook for 2 hours until the meat is soft and tender. Serve the stew over a bed of wide egg noodles.

Icebox Cake

This was one of the few things my dad could cook. And I've recently discovered that it was the only thing a lot of my friend's dad's could cook as well. I've adapted it just a little because that's what younger generations are supposed to do. Don't be surprised if, like Proust's madelaines, this dessert induces spontaneous joy as guests remember their own dads presenting it proudly at the dinner table. This dish should really sit in the refrigerator overnight, so keep that in mind when preparing this meal.

½ cup whipping cream

½ cup confectioner's sugar

1 cup skim milk ricotta cheese

1 tablespoon Amaretto or Kaluha

1 teaspoon vanilla

1 box Nabisco chocolate wafer cookies

Cocoa for dusting (approximately 2 tablespoons)

Fresh berries such as strawberries, blueberries, or rasberries for garnish

Music

This meal has no distinct ethnic origins. It's just good food. So put on some good music. *Charlie Parker with Strings*, some Sam Cooke, or Diane Schur. The Beatles' *Rubber Soul*, *Smokey Robinson's Greatest Hits*, or Glenn Gould playing Bach. You get the idea.

1. Before starting, put a medium mixing bowl in the freezer for 1/2 hour. Remove the bowl and immediately use it to beat the cream with an electric mixer on high speed until it forms stiff peaks. Add the confectioner's sugar and continue beating until it is incorporated into the cream, about 20 seconds.

2. Place the ricotta into a large mixing bowl. Using a rubber spatula, fold the whipped cream into the ricotta. Stir in the Amaretto (or Kaluha) and vanilla.

3. Gently spread about 2 tablespoons of the ricotta mixture on one of the wafers, being careful not to break it. Place another wafer on top of the ricotta to make a sandwich. Spread 2 more tablespoons on the second wafer and place another wafer on top of that. Repeat until you have a stack of 5 wafers, at which

point you'll need to lay the wafers on their side and build the cake horizontally. Place a 16-inch length of aluminum foil on a baking sheet. Place the same length of plastic wrap over the foil. Continue assembling the cake on the plastic wrap.

4. When you've used up all the wafers, use a rubber spatula to ice the cake with the remaining ricotta mixture. Gently roll the cake in the plastic and foil and place the baking sheet with the cake in the refrigerator for at least 4 hours, preferably, overnight. To serve, remove the cake from the freezer and let it soften for 20 minutes before slicing at an angle into 2-inch pieces. Measure a few tablespoons of cocoa powder into a small strainer. Gently tap the strainer over the cake slices to dust with cocoa. Serve the cake garnished with fresh berries.

Easy Dinner for Eight

Recipes make 8 servings

There are so many reasons to have a dinner party for eight; you've just recovered the stools of your rumpus room jungle bar in leopard Naugahyde; you got a new Ping-Pong table and it's time to host a tournament; it's been 20 years since you last played strip poker; it's been a *week* since you last played strip poker; friends have recently purchased a large condo in a fancy ski resort and you're looking for some *quid pro quo* this winter.

Whatever the reason, even if it's something as banal as having dinner with people you enjoy being with, this menu will unquestionably please and impress them. The dishes have a distinctly Mediterranean flavor with their particular combination of spices and ingredients. North African influences show up in the use of dried fruits and curry. The salad has traces of Sicilian cuisine. The humus dip is of Middle Eastern origin, and I just made up the dessert because it seemed to go with the rest of the food and was easy to make.

MENU

Humus
Fennel, Red Onion, and Orange Salad
Mediterranean Chicken over Couscous
Sautéed Apples and Vanilla Ice Cream

Humus

Makes 8 appetizer servings

When I lived near Atlantic Avenue in Brooklyn, the New York Mecca for Middle Eastern food and spices, I frequently stopped in one of the many restaurants for a quick fix of humus and baba ganoush. A bowl of olives would go well with this dish.

One 15-ounce can chickpeas, drained

2 tablespoons sesame tahini (also called sesame paste)

1 clove garlic, coarsely chopped

2 tablespoons fresh lemon juice

1 tablespoon olive oil

1 teaspoon salt

2 tablespoons cold water

1 pinch of paprika for garnish

4 rounds of pita bread cut into eighths and/or 12 ounces crisp flat breads

Note

If you are using a blender, you will need to add the two tablespoons of water along with the other ingredients.

1. Place the chickpeas, tahini, garlic, lemon juice, olive oil, and salt in the bowl of a food processor or blender and process until smooth, about 2 minutes. If the mixture seems unsuitably stiff or coarse to use as a dip, add the cold water, one tablespoon at a time.

2. Sprinkle paprika over the top as a garnish and serve with the pita bread.

Fennel, Red Onion, and Orange Salad

Makes 8 servings

The idea of this exotic salad might take a little getting used to, but the flavor certainly won't.

2 medium fennel bulbs	3 tablespoons orange juice
6 naval oranges, peeled	¼ cup olive oil
1 small red onion, peeled	½ teaspoon salt
3 tablespoons balsamic vinegar	

1. Trim the bottoms off the fennel bulbs, cut them in half lengthwise, and then cut across each half into the thinnest possible slices. Transfer to a salad bowl.

2. Cut the oranges in half lengthwise, and then into medium slices, about ⅓ inch. Don't cut them too thin, or they will fall apart. Cut the onion in half lengthwise, then lengthwise again into the thinnest slices you can get. Transfer the oranges and the onion slices to the salad bowl.

3. Whisk together the balsamic vinegar, orange juice, olive oil, and salt in a bowl and pour it over the salad. Toss the salad and serve.

Music

Given the sum of the North African influences in this meal, some Um Kalthum might be in order. But even though Um is reputed to have sold more records than anyone else in music history, she is still an acquired taste. Guitarist Otmar Liebert combines almost as many musical influences as this meal combines Mediterranean influences.

For a French feel, try recordings by such cabaret legends as Yves Montand, Jacques Brel, or Edith Piaf. There are also collections of French dance hall music from the '30s that will immediately transport you to Paris.

Note

You can make the salad up to two hours before the party and store it, covered with plastic wrap, in the refrigerator. Wait to add the dressing just before serving.

Fun and Games

There's a chance that this Mediterranean meal might spur some of your guests to recount details of their trips abroad. This can be particularly painful if you yourself haven't been to Europe for a while or, alas, never at all. If this is the case, here's what you should say to quickly quiet them down. (This version works for France and Italy. Just choose the appropriate selection within the parentheses. You can also adapt it to suit your vengeful needs.)

YOU: So, Phyllis and Mort, you just got back from _____ (France/Italy).

THEM: Yes. It was wonderful.

YOU: That's just great. There's a fabulous little town in the _____ (South/North). Did you happen to get there? It's called _____ (Joufool/Tuopozzo).

THEM: No.

YOU: (*shocked*) No??!!

THEM: Well, we only had a few days.

YOU: Still, not to go there. Tsk, tsk, tsk. Such a shame. It's the perfect _____ (French/Italian) town. It's up on a hill, surrounded by _____ (vineyards/olive groves). It has mazes of winding streets. No tourists. A wonderful little museum with a fantastic (Delacroix/Tintoretto).

THEM: It sounds ideal.

YOU: It is. And believe it or not, it has absolutely the best restaurant in all of _____ (France; Italy).

THEM: Really?

YOU: Yes. It's where _____ (Jacques Pepin/Marcella Hazan) goes when _____ (he/she) wants a good meal.

THEM: Oh. That sounds wonderful.

YOU: (*with great remorse*) My God, it is! Such a *shame* you didn't get there. The _____ (pike quenelles/lobster and porcini risotto)—to die for.

THEM: Oh we love that food.

YOU: I know. But that's just for starters. There's another specialty: _____ (roast partridge/gnocchi and truffles).

THEM: Agh.

YOU: There's more.

THEM: Enough. Please.

YOU: But I want you to *know* how much you *missed* . For the main course, the chef, _____ (Paul/Paolo), brings this platter of veal cutlets smothered in _____ (garlic and butter/garlic and oil) that simply melt in your mouth.

THEM: Stop!

YOU: No! The _____ (mache/arugala) is grown in a garden out back. The _____ (Camembert/Tallegio) is from a local dairy. And the dessert—_____ (pear tart Tatin/fresh figs with zabaglione)—is made with fruit freshly picked that morning.

THEM: It sounds...unbelievable. What's the name of the restaurant?

YOU: No name. You just go to the center of town, walk behind the _____ (Cathedral/Duomo), down a winding alley, through a 19th-century hidden sculpture garden, along an 18th-century cobblestone street, past a row of quaint 17th-century houses, and it's just on the edge of a 16th-century square. It's like you're stepping back in time.

THEM: (*collective sigh*)

YOU: Oh, and did I mention? The meal only costs about $14.

THEM: For one?

YOU: No, for two.

THEM: We feel sick.

YOU: Oh, I didn't mean...

THEM: No. It was like our trip was a waste of time.

YOU: Yes, perhaps it was.

THEM: Hopefully, we'll get there next time.

YOU: Yes. Next time. If it hasn't been discovered by then. By the way, this place only serves lunch. Wait until I tell you what you missed for dinner.

Mediterranean Chicken Over Couscous

Makes 8 servings

The hint of Arabic flavors and the dried fruit give this dish an exotic flavor, and once you have all the spices assembled, it couldn't be easier to make. Well, it could be easier to make if, say, I were to come to your house and make it for you.

2 tablespoons curry powder

1 tablespoon dried coriander

1 teaspoon ground cumin

1/2 teaspoon Chinese five spice powder

1/2 teaspoon ground ginger

1 dash cayenne

2 tablespoons olive oil

8 chicken breasts with the bone and skin

8 chicken thighs

1/2 cup canned chicken broth, or 1/2 cup water and 1 chicken bouillon cube

2 large onions, thinly sliced

1 tart apple, peeled, cored, and thinly sliced

4 stalks celery, cut into 1/2-inch slices

6 garlic cloves, coarsely chopped

1/2 cup sherry

16 baby carrots

16 large pitied prunes

2 packages frozen artichoke hearts or two 12-ounce cans of artichoke hearts in water, drained

1 teaspoon salt

1. Preheat the oven to 375°F. In a small bowl, mix together all the spices. Pull back the skin from the chicken pieces and rub the meat with the spice mixture—about 1/2 teaspoon per piece. Put the skin back in place and save the remaining spice mixture.

2. Measure the chicken broth or water and bouillon cube into a small saucepan and heat it slowly over a low heat until the bouillon dissolves while you are preparing the rest of the ingredients. If it comes to a simmer, turn off the heat.

3. Heat the olive oil in a large, heavy skillet until it is very hot, about 1½ minutes, spreading the oil so that it evenly glazes the bottom. Add 4 of the chicken breasts and cook until the skin is nicely brown, about 3 minutes. Turn and cook 3 minutes more. Transfer the breasts to a platter and repeat with the remaining 4 breasts. You will not need to add more oil.

4. Reduce the heat to medium high and add the onions, apple, and celery. Cook, stirring frequently, until the onions are soft, about 5 minutes. Add the garlic and the remaining spice mixture and cook one minute more, again stirring frequently. Add the sherry and cook until the liquid is reduced by half.

5. Transfer the onion mixture to the bottom of a 12x19-inch casserole pan. Add the carrots, prunes, frozen artichoke hearts, and salt and then mix together. Lay the chicken pieces on top. Cover the casserole tightly with aluminum foil. Bake for 40 minutes or until the breasts are cooked through.

6. Serve on a large platter over a mound of couscous or on individual plates.

Couscous

Makes 8 servings

Couscous is a traditional North African grain made from semolina flour. It cooks very quickly and needs to be monitored carefully, so it doesn't become one big globular mess.

3 cups canned chicken broth, or 3 cups water and 3 bouillon cubes

3 cups couscous

1. Bring the chicken broth or water and bouillon cubes to a boil over a high heat, stirring so the bouillon is dissolved. When the liquid is boiling, add the couscous and immediately stir well. Cover the pot and continue cooking for 1 minute. Then turn off the heat (electric stove users need to move the pot off the hot coil) and let it rest, covered, for 5 more minutes.

2. Transfer the couscous to a platter or individual plates and fluff gently with a fork before spooning the chicken and sauce over it.

Note

Couscous should be served right after you make it. The best plan is to bring the water to a simmer as your guests are enjoying the first course. Then, just before serving the main course, cook the couscous. In the few minutes' lull, the guests can pour themselves some wine and talk about great meals they've had in Europe.

Sautéed Apples and Vanilla Ice Cream

Makes 8 servings

After you've peeled the apples (or worked out a suitable arrangement for one of your kids to do it), this dessert goes together quickly. It can be enhanced by warming the apples in the microwave or reheating them in a skillet before serving.

7 tart apples, such as Granny
   Smith or Gala, peeled
2 tablespoons fresh lemon juice
½ cup sugar
1 teaspoon cinnamon

3 tablespoons butter
½ cup canned cranberry jelly
1 teaspoon chopped fresh ginger
2 pints best vanilla ice cream

1. Cut the apples into quarters. Trim the core from each quarter and cut in half lengthwise. Place the apple slices as you cut them in a mixing bowl with the lemon juice. Periodically toss the apple slices in the lemon juice to keep them from turning brown. When all the apples are sliced, sprinkle the sugar and cinnamon over them and toss so they are evenly coated.

2. Place a large skillet over medium-high heat. Add the butter to the pan and as it starts sizzling, spread it so that it evenly glazes the bottom. Add the apples and cook, stirring often, until they are soft but not mushy and lightly brown. Transfer the apples to a bowl.

3. Reduce the heat to low and add the cranberry jelly and ginger to the skillet. Cook until the jelly is reduced by half.

4. To serve, arrange 8 dessert bowls on the counter, put a scoop of vanilla ice cream in each bowl, and cover with the apple slices. Then pour the warm cranberry/ginger sauce through a strainer onto the apple slices.

drinks

The old rule about white wine only with chicken doesn't need to be followed religiously anymore. This is especially true of a chicken dish that features the kind of spices this one does. A California Zinfandel would be a good choice to compliment the chicken, since it has a slight hint of spiciness of its own. Some Zinfandels to look for are Gallo-Sonoma's "Frei Ranch"; Hidden Cellars' "Old Vine"; Renwood's "Old Vine"; Seghesio's "Sonoma"; or the Zinfandel from the Talus vineyard, which has a deep, rich flavor and is also an excellent value.

"Jamaica?" "No, she wanted to."
~A Caribbean Feast

Recipes make 8 servings

It's summer. It's your first weekend after the kids have left for camp. What better way to celebrate than to invite over three other similarly liberated couples to indulge in tall glasses of frosty rum and fruit drinks. Then you can treat them to this spicy, sumptuous feast that, if you do nothing else for the next two months, will make it the most memorable summer since you frolicked in Europe after graduating college.

This meal is perhaps the most difficult in the book. It definitely requires some cooking. But because you have no responsibilities this weekend, you easily can spend an afternoon in the kitchen. Caribbean food is meant for friends, for feasting together. The flavors are exotic and surprising, and the *piononos* will instantly become your favorite appetizer.

About Caribbean Cuisine

Caribbean cooking emphasizes a combination of sweet and sour flavors, relying on lots of onions and garlic and lime to supply the tanginess. It's very refreshing food, never subtle, yet not overpowering. The boneless roast pork loin is the centerpiece of the meal. Be sure to have plenty of drinks to accompany the succulent appetizers, although I suggest that you make them on the weak side, because people have a tendency to have more than they should with such easy-to-drink cocktails.

MENU

Hard and Soft Tropical Drinks
Dr. No's Fish Chowder
Piononos
Jerk Chicken Kebobs
Day-O Roast Loin of Pork
Festive Coconut Rice
Fresh Papaya, Mango, and
Pineapple with Lemon Sorbet

Strawberry and Mango
Frozen Daiquiris

Makes 4 servings

These drinks are not too strong. Because they taste so good, it's hard to stop. This way, you can drink more of them.

1 mango, peeled and flesh removed
　　from pit
6 strawberries, stems removed
4 ounces light or dark rum
1 ounce Cointreau or Triple Sec

1 lime, peeled
1 teaspoon sugar
2 cups crushed ice

Put everything in a blender and puree at highest speed for 30 to 40 seconds until it is smoothly blended.

TIP

If you want to make these for the kids, substitute 1 cup of pineapple juice for the liquor.

Dr. No's Fish Chowder

Makes 8 servings

The addition of a bit of rum and a hint of Pickapeppa sauce makes this chowder distinctly Jamaican. Like many Caribbean dishes, this one has lots of ingredients, but they all go in one pot, so the preparation is not as difficult as it might seem at first. This soup was Dr. No's favorite dish after he settled in the Caribbean. He, of course, didn't need pot holders.

3 slices slab bacon or 5 slices packaged bacon cut into ¹/₂-inch pieces

1 medium onion, finely chopped

1 medium carrot, peeled and cut into ¹/₂-inch chunks

2 celery ribs, cut in half lengthwise, then into ¹/₂-inch slices

3 garlic cloves, minced

4 cups canned chicken broth

2 cups bottled clam juice

2 cups canned crushed tomatoes

¹/₄ cup dark rum

¹/₄ cup sherry or port

1¹/₂ pounds snapper fillets or other firm-fleshed whitefish, cut into ¹/₂-inch chunks

2 medium yams, peeled and cut into ¹/₂-inch cubes

1 bay leaf

2 tablespoons Pickapeppa sauce (see Note)

1 teaspoon salt

¹/₂ teaspoon cayenne pepper

1. Place a heavy-bottomed soup pot over medium-high heat and let it get hot, about 1 minute. Add the bacon and cook, stirring often until it is almost crispy, about 2 minutes. Pour out most of the grease and then add the onions, carrots, and celery and cook until they are soft, about 5 minutes, stirring frequently. Add the garlic and cook 1 minute more.

2. Add the broth, clam juice, tomatoes, rum, and sherry (or port) and bring the mixture to a boil. Then add the fish pieces, yams, bay leaf, Pickapeppa, salt, and cayenne pepper.

3. When the liquid returns to a boil, reduce the heat to low, cover, and simmer for 20 to 25 minutes, until the yams are cooked through. Serve with crusty peasant bread.

Note

If you can't find Pickapeppa sauce, use 2 tablespoons of Worcestershire and ¹/₂ teaspoon of allspice.

Piononos

Makes 8 servings as an appetizer

These delectable appetizers are made by wrapping a slice of ripe plantain around a savory filling and then frying them in corn oil. They can be made up to four hours ahead of time and then reheated before the party. They also require the most work of any dish in this meal, so if you're not feeling adventurous, just serve the jerk chicken. If you want a truly authentic taste of the Islands, however, give these a try. They're worth it. One guest swore it was the best thing she ever put in her mouth.

3 large ripe plantains
2 tablespoons butter
2 tablespoons corn oil
½ pound lean ground sirloin
1 small grated onion
2 garlic cloves, minced
2 tablespoons all-purpose flour
1 cup canned chopped tomatoes

6 large black olives, pitted and chopped finely
1 teaspoon salt
1 teaspoon malt vinegar
½ teaspoon cayenne pepper
Corn oil for frying (about 1 cup)
4 eggs

Note

You can prepare the piononos through step 5 up to several hours before the party. Store them on a waxed-paper-lined cookie sheet, cover with plastic wrap, and refrigerate until you're ready to finish cooking them.

1. Peel two of the plantains and cut them lengthwise into 4 to 5 strips, about ¼ inch thick. The third plantain is in case you mess up.

2. Place a large frying pan over medium-high heat. Add 1 tablespoon of butter and ½ tablespoon of oil to the pan. As the butter starts sizzling, spread it so that it evenly glazes the bottom. Arrange 4 of the plantain slices in the pan and cook them until they start to brown, about 2 to 3 minutes. Then turn them and cook them 2 to 3 minutes more. Transfer the cooked slices onto a paper towel to soak up any excess oil. Add the remaining tablespoon of butter and another ½ tablespoon of oil to the pan and repeat the process with the remaining 4 slices of plantain, transferring them to the paper towel as well.

3. Increase the heat to high and add the remaining 1 tablespoon of oil to the pan, spreading it so it glazes the bottom. Add the chopped sirloin and onion and cook until the meat loses its pinkness. Press the meat down with a fork to break it up. Add the garlic and cook 1 minute more. Sprinkle the flour over the mixture, stir it in, and cook 2 minutes more, stirring frequently.

4. Add the crushed tomato, olives, salt, vinegar, and pepper and cook until the liquid thickens, about 3 minutes. Transfer the meat mixture to a medium bowl and let it cool for 10 minutes before filling the plantains.

5. Shape a plantain strip into a ring and secure it with a toothpick. Spoon in enough of the meat mixture to fill the ring to the top. Repeat with the remaining plantains.

6. Beat the 4 eggs in a medium bowl. Wipe out the frying pan and add enough oil to fill it 1 inch high. Place the pan on high heat and let it get hot, about 2 minutes. While the pan is heating, place 4 of the *piononos* in the bowl with the eggs, spooning some of the eggs over them so that they are entirely coated. Lift them individually cradled in two spoons and place them gently in the hot oil. (Do not drop them in the pan as the oil may splatter.) · Cook them for 2 minutes until the bottom is golden brown. Turn each *pionono* gently with the two spoons and cook 1 minute more. Transfer them to some paper towel and then serve.

A Glossary of Caribbean Food

Coo Coo: A baked pudding made from cornmeal and okra.

Mofungo: Classic Puerto Rican spread made from half-ripened plantains mashed with pork cracklings and garlic.

Pepper Pot: A traditional chicken stew from Trinidad seasoned with pigs feet and cassava juice (cassareep).

Jerk Chicken Kebobs

Makes 8 servings

This dish involves marinating the chicken for one to four hours, and then simply broiling it. With the recent interest in Jamaican food, several fine jerk sauces now are available in specialty shops and even in supermarkets. Or you can make your own (recipe follows).

2 cups homemade or bottled jerk marinade (recipe follows)
½ pound skinless and boneless chicken breasts cut into 1½-inch pieces

16 bamboo skewers

1. Place the chicken in a medium-size stainless steel or glass bowl and pour on 1½ cups of the sauce. Mix the chicken so that all the pieces are completely coated with sauce. Then cover the bowl with plastic wrap and place it in the refrigerator for at least one hour and not more than four. While the chicken is marinating, put the skewers in a bowl and cover them with hot water to soak until you're ready to use them. This will keep them from burning.

2. Preheat the broiler or grill. Place three chicken pieces on each skewer and lay the kebobs on a broiler tray. Discard the marinade. Broil the kebobs about 4 inches from the flame until they brown, about 3 minutes. Turn and broil for 2 minutes more until they are just cooked through. Serve with additional sauce on the side.

Jerk Sauce

Makes 2 cups

This sauce traditionally was used in the process of drying meats before long sea voyages. Now it's used as a pungent and spicy marinade and barbecue sauce.

¼ **cup water**

¼ **cup ketchup**

¼ **cup malt vinegar**

¼ **cup Pickapeppa or Worcestershire sauce**

2 tablespoons vegetable oil

2 tablespoons sugar

1 tablespoon salt

1 teaspoon garlic powder

1 teaspoon onion powder

1 teaspoon allspice

½ **teaspoon cinnamon**

½ **teaspoon Tabasco sauce**

1. Mix all the ingredients together in a medium size stainless steel or glass bowl.

2. Refrigerate the sauce until it's ready to be used.

Fun and Games

Before dessert, it's time for LIMBO! Get out the broomstick, put on your old Harry Belafonte albums or the calypso CD you bought for the evening, and see who can get down lowest under the bar. The basic rules are that two people hold a stick under which the others must pass without bending forward, sideways, or letting their hands touch the floor (which, if you haven't been paying attention, leaves only bending backward.) Begin with the bar about chest high. If you and your friends have been working out as rigorously as I have these past few years, the starting height should knock everyone out of the competition. For a demonstration, rent the James Bond movie *Dr. No* before the party.

Day-O Roast Loin of Pork

Makes 8 servings

Named after the Belefonte tune, which was one of my favorite songs when I was a kid. This is a simple preparation. The only catch is making sure that you don't overcook the meat.

1 cup light brown sugar

½ medium onion, grated

2 tablespoons dark rum

6 garlic cloves, minced

1 teaspoon ground ginger

½ teaspoon ground allspice

½ teaspoon cayenne pepper

1 boneless loin of pork, 2½ to 3 pounds

2 cups canned chicken broth

3 tablespoons fresh lime juice

1. Preheat your oven to 350°F. In a medium mixing bowl, use the back of a wooden spoon to make a paste out of the sugar, grated onion, rum, garlic, ground ginger, and allspice. You might have to use your fingers a bit, too.

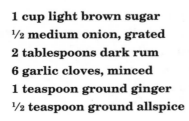

Note

If you're not sure if the loin is done, cut into it at its thickest point. If the center is white and opaque, it's done.

2. Rub the paste entirely over the pork loin. Place the loin on a rack set in a roasting pan. Add the chicken broth to the bottom of the pan and place it on the center rack of the oven. Cook for 1 hour and 25 minutes, or until the internal temperature reaches 150°F to 160°F on a meat thermometer. You might need to add some water to the bottom of the pan while the loin is roasting. Check after 45 minutes.

3. When the loin is done, remove it from the rack and let it rest 5 minutes before slicing. Meanwhile, spoon off any fat from the pan drippings by tilting the pan slightly and letting the juices collect in a corner. Remember to use a pot holder. Add the lime juice to the drippings and stir together. Season with a little salt if necessary. Transfer the sauce to a gravy boat or bowl.

4. Cut the loin into 1-inch slices and serve with the sauce made from the pan gravy and lime juice.

Festive Coconut Rice

Makes 8 servings

The addition of coconut milk gives this rice a silky texture. Make sure that you use unsweetened coconut milk for this recipe (look for the low-fat version now available) as opposed to the sweetened coconut milk essential to piña coladas.

½ **red bell pepper, diced**

1 **tablespoon butter**

1½ **cups white rice preferably Basmati**

1½ **cups unsweetened coconut milk**

2½ **cups canned chicken broth**

1 **tablespoon curry powder**

1 **teaspoon ground ginger**

½ **teaspoon cayenne**

2 **scallions, green parts only, cut into ½-inch rounds**

1. Place a large heavy-bottom frying pan on medium-high heat and add the butter. When it stops sizzling, add the red pepper and cook, stirring often, until it softens, about 2 minutes.

2. Add the rice to the pan along with the coconut milk, broth, curry, ginger, cayenne, and salt and stir everything together with a wooden spoon. When the liquid comes to a boil, reduce the heat to low and cover the pan. Cook until the rice is just cooked through, about 18 minutes. (It's wise to set a timer.) Serve garnished with the scallions.

Cucumber Salad

Makes 8 servings

It's popular on the Islands to throw together a simple, light salad like this one to help cool the tongue during the meal.

2 cucumbers or 1 English
  (seedless) cucumber

3 tablespoons fresh lime juice
  (about 2 limes)

1 teaspoon salt

A sprinkling of red pepper flakes
  (about ¼ teaspoon)

1. Peel the cucumbers and slice them down the middle lengthwise. Use the tip of a teaspoon to scrape out the seeds.

2. Cut the cukes into thin slices, about ¼ inch, and put them in a medium stainless steel or glass mixing bowl. Add the lime juice, salt, and pepper flakes. Toss together to coat the cucumber slices. Refrigerate until ready to serve.

Music

Caribbean music is imbued with a strong beat and a joyful exuberance. It's happy music, meant to be played loud, especially at an important feast. And because the kids aren't home, do it. Check out recordings by the following groups:

Toots and the Maytals—*Greatest Hits*
Dominican Republic National Steel Band
Celia Cruz
The Kingstonians
Desmond Dekker
Bob Marley

Fresh Papaya, Mango, and Pineapple with Lemon Sorbet

Makes 8 servings

Fresh fruits are abundant on the Islands and are eaten with almost every meal. Exotic fruits like akee are a rarity except where they grow. But you should be able to find some mangoes and papayas for dessert.

Papaya

Most likely, you will have access to yellow papayas, although the larger red papaya also is popular on the Islands.

A ripe papaya should be a deep yellow and feel very soft but not mushy.

Peel the papaya with a sharp paring knife or peeler and then cut it in half lengthwise. Scoop out the seeds and save. A few can be used as garnish. For serving, cut each half lengthwise into quarters.

Mango

For me, a cold, ripe mango is one of the most sublime eating experiences.

A fully ripe mango has a deep purplish color with yellow hues. Like the papaya, it should be very soft but with no mushy spots.

Peel the mango with a sharp paring knife or peeler. Mangoes have a large, flat pit about an inch wide that runs across the fruit. This allows you to get only two clean slices. Try cutting into the mango lengthwise to slice off about ⅓ from one side. If you hit the pit right away, rotate it slightly and try again. After slicing your first one, you'll know exactly what I mean. Buy an extra mango for practice and to snack on while you're making dessert. Cut each large slice in half or thirds.

Pineapple

A ripe pineapple should be slightly firm with some give to it. It shouldn't be soft—otherwise, it's probably overripe. The outside should be a dark brownish green. If you can pull out one of the bottom leaves easily, then it's ready. If you have to yank the leaves out, it needs a day or two on top of the refrigerator.

Cut across the pineapple about ½ inch below the top. Stand the pineapple on its bottom and cut it lengthwise in half. Then cut each half lengthwise in quarters. Trim the triangular strip of core from each slice. Cut the meat from the skin and then slice these into 1-inch pieces.

Presenting the Dessert

Place a scoop of sorbet in the center of a dessert plate. Arrange the fruit slices around it and garnish with 4 or 5 of the papaya seeds.

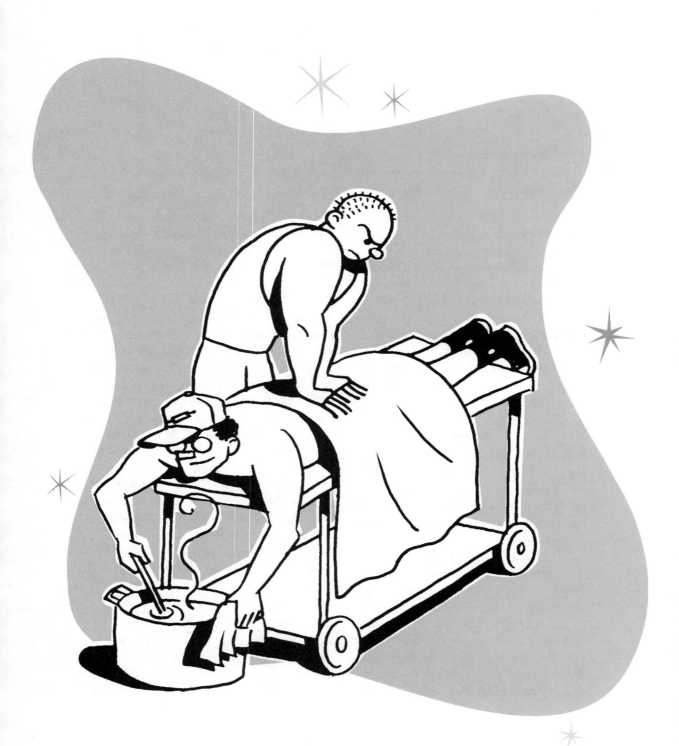

Spa Dinner for Eight

Recipes make 8 servings

One major trend in food since the '80s has been toward a paucity of fat—fruit for breakfast, vegetables for lunch, a bowl of steam for dinner. *Spa cuisine*, however, has expanded the culinary possibilities of cooking with little or no fat. Poaching foods in stock or vegetable reductions has replaced sautéing them in butter or oil. Chicken, fish, and vegetables have replaced meat as the main course. Pureed vegetables give sauces body and tone, replacing the cream. Spa chefs have found new ways to infuse a dish with flavor, often looking to exotic ingredients and compelling combinations of tastes. That kind of approach is explored here in this elegant yet easy-to-prepare dinner.

MeNU

Butternut Squash and Apple Soup
Fillet of Sole or Flounder with
Red Pepper Puree
Chicken with Pineapple
Sorbet with Fresh Berries and Fruit

Butternut Squash and Apple Soup

Makes 8 servings

This light, creamy soup is actually made without any cream or butter. The apple serves to sweeten it a bit.

1 tart apple, such as Granny Smith or Gala, peeled, cored, and sliced

1 medium onion, peeled and sliced

1 butternut squash, peeled, seeded, and cut into 2-inch pieces

4 cups chicken broth

1 teaspoon salt

1 teaspoon cinnamon

A pinch of nutmeg

Plain nonfat yogurt

1. Place a 3½-quart saucepan on a medium-high heat. Spray the bottom with oil, add the onions and apples, and cook, stirring continuously, until they soften, about 4 minutes. Add the pieces of squash and chicken broth and bring the liquid to a boil over high heat. When it boils, cover the pot, reduce the heat to low, and simmer for 15 minutes or until the squash is cooked through.

Note

You also can use a food processor fitted with the metal blade to puree the soup, but a blender works best.

You can make the soup up to a month in advance. Let it cool completely before storing it in the freezer in a well-sealed plastic container.

2. Use a ladle to transfer half the soup to the bowl of a blender. Make sure that you have equal amounts of liquid and solid. The soup won't puree properly with too much of either. Puree, being careful not to be splattered by the hot liquid, until the soup is smooth and creamy. Transfer to a second saucepan or mixing bowl. Finish pureeing the remainder of the soup.

3. Return the soup to the heat and stir in the salt, cinnamon, and nutmeg. Correct for seasoning and heat through. Serve the soup in shallow soup bowls garnished with a dollop of yogurt and a pinch of cinnamon or nutmeg. Or you can follow the more detailed garnishing notes at the end of this chapter.

Fillet of Sole or Flounder with Red Pepper Puree

Makes 8 servings

One of the more generous aspects of spa cuisine is that it encourages serving a number of small courses, each with its own distinct flavor. This is a light second course which, in addition to its subtle yet distinctive flavor, emphasizes a colorful presentation. It's simply too trés chic.

4 red bell peppers, cored and seeded

½ cup white wine

Salt and pepper

Vegetable oil spray

8 small boneless sole or flounder fillets, about 1½ pounds total

¼ cup chicken broth

¼ cup fresh lemon juice

Fresh parsley or basil for garnish

1. Cut the peppers into quarters and put them in a saucepan with ¼ cup of white wine. Cover the pan and bring the liquid to a boil, and then quickly reduce the heat to low and steam the peppers until they are soft, about 30 minutes.

2. When the peppers are soft, use a slotted spoon to transfer them to the bowl of a processor fitted with a metal blade or a blender. Process or blend until the mixture is smooth, adding some of the cooking liquid as needed. Season the sauce with salt and pepper and transfer to a small saucepan so that it can be reheated just before serving.

3. Preheat the oven to 350°F. Spray a large baking pan with oil, arrange the fish fillets in one layer, and sprinkle them with salt and pepper.

4. Mix together the remaining ¼ cup of wine, chicken broth, and lemon juice in a small bowl and pour over the fish. Season the fish lightly with salt and pepper. Spray one side of a piece of aluminum foil with oil and gently cover the pan, oiled side down, pinching the sides to make a secure seal.

5. Place the pan in the oven and poach the fillets until they are just cooked through, 8 to 10 minutes. Place a fish fillet in the center of each plate. Spoon a few tablespoons of sauce over the fish and garnish with a sprig of parsley or fresh basil.

Note

You can prepare steps 1 and 2 of this recipe the morning of the party. Store the red pepper sauce in a plastic container in the refrigerator and reheat it over low heat before serving. You can arrange the fish on the baking pan, cover it with plastic, and store it in the refrigerator.

Chicken with Pineapple

Makes 8 servings

Pounding the chicken breasts until they are quite thin allows them to cook more quickly with very little oil. It also helps to use a nonstick pan. If you don't have a real meat pounder and refuse to shell out the few bucks required to buy one, you can flatten the chicken with the side of a can or the bottom of a soda bottle. Just don't hurt yourself.

½ cup fresh lemon juice

2 tablespoons chopped fresh cilantro

2 tablespoons chopped parsley

2 tablespoons chopped scallion greens

1 cup pineapple juice

1 tablespoon orange marmalade

Vegetable oil spray

1 teaspoon finely chopped fresh ginger

8 skinless and boneless chicken breasts, pounded to about 1/4 inch thick

drinks

Wine Selections

A well-chilled California Chardonnay or French Muscadet would go well with this meal. If you prefer red with chicken and fish, as some people do, go with a Beaujolais—especially a Beaujolais Nouveau served lightly chilled.

1. Preheat the oven to 250°F. Mix the lemon juice, cilantro, parsley, and scallions together in a small mixing bowl.

2. Put the pineapple juice, marmalade, and ginger in a small, non-reactive saucepan. Bring the liquid to a boil over high heat, and then lower the heat to medium and cook until the liquid is reduced by half, stirring occasionally, about 8 minutes.

3. Place a large, nonstick frying pan on a high heat, spray it with a light coating of oil, and let it get hot. Place 4 chicken breasts in the pan and cook until the bottom is lightly brown, 3 to 4 minutes. Turn and cook 2 to 3 minutes more. Transfer the breasts to a platter, cover with foil, and put them in the warm oven while you cook the remaining 4 breasts in the same way. Transfer these to the platter as well.

4. Add the lemon mixture to the hot pan, stirring continuously until it reduces by half. Add the pineapple sauce to the pan and stir it into the lemon mixture. To serve, place one chicken breast on each plate and spoon a few tablespoons of sauce over it. Garnish with a sprig of fresh herbs and a melange of steamed vegetables, such as snow peas, baby carrots, broccoli, and cauliflower.

Sorbet with Fresh Berries and Fruit

Makes 8 servings

Desserts that try to be low fat or nonfat interpretations of normal (fatty, gooey, decadent) ones tend to be a little on the disappointing side. So better to go with a dessert that is what it's supposed to be. Mango or passion fruit sorbet will compliment the color of the berries, and a little kiwi arranged neatly around the plate will give it that spa look.

**3 pints sorbet, preferably
3 different flavors**

1 bunch mint

At least 2 of the following:

**1 pint strawberries, stemmed and
cut in half lengthwise**

1 pint blueberries

½ pint raspberries

½ pint blackberries

**4 kiwis, peeled, cut in half length-
wise, then into ¼ inch slices**

1. Place one small scoop of each flavor on each dessert plate. Arrange 5 or 6 kiwi slices around the edge of the plate.

2. Arrange some berries in little clusters around the sorbet. Garnish with a sprig of mint.

Getting the Spa Look

Drama is the hallmark of spa presentation. Sometimes this is the result of contrasting colors, sometimes by assembling the food into compelling structures, and sometimes by putting a teensy bit of food on a huge plate.

To do up the butternut squash soup, you'll need a small squeeze bottle, about 4 ounces, which you can get in a drugstore (the kind commonly used for coloring hair). Fill the bottle with nonfat sour cream. Squeeze three lines of the sour cream across the center of the bowl, about 1 inch apart. Do this lightly so they rest on the surface of the soup. Run the tip of a knife blade perpendicularly through the sour cream at ½-inch intervals. The results should resemble three upside down EKG readouts.

Use 3-inch lengths of chives to garnish the fish, arranging two of them in an X-shape across the red pepper.

Steamed colorful vegetables will work to garnish the chicken. Imagining the plate as a clock, make small clusters with a snow pea, baby carrot, and cauliflower floret on the very edge of the plate at 12:00, 3:00, 6:00, and 9:00.

Killing a Rainy Afternoon Baking with Your Kids

Recipes make at least 8 servings

It's a rainy Sunday and you're not sure what to do with the kids. There are puddles on the miniature golf course, so that's out. You just went bowling yesterday and you're now finally standing up straight again. The kids have watched every appropriate video twice and you're not ready for them to see anything with Freddy, Jason, or Chuckie. The racetrack is closed for the season and the batting cage...well, how many times can you go to the batting cage?

So what better, more productive way to spend the afternoon than baking with the kids? Not dainty baking. Not lacy cookies or petite pastries filled with cream, but rugged baking. The kind of baking Lee Marvin would do. Or Broderick Crawford. Or Charles Bronson on his day off. This is baking that requires kneading and pounding the dough, beating the batter. It's tough, fun work. But you also can make a party out of it. Throw flour at each other. Create rude sculptures with some extra bits of bread dough—odd, alien-looking cookies like something stuck to the bottom of Sigourney Weaver's spaceship when she returns to earth. Make it fun. When you are done, you can finish off the day by sneaking what you've baked into the movie theater and devouring it there, to the consternation and envy of everyone sitting around you.

MENU

Banana Chocolate Chip Mega Muffins
Whole Wheat Bread
Chocolate Cookies
Oatmeal Raisin Bread

The batting order for the afternoon baking follows:

1. Preheat the oven to 350°F. Make the batter for the whole wheat bread and let it start rising.

2. While the bread is rising, prepare and bake the muffins. This will give you and the kids something to munch on for the rest of the day.

3. Make the batter for the chocolate cookies and let it start to chill in the refrigerator. The whole wheat dough for the bread should have risen sufficiently by now, so beat it down and shape it into loaves.

4. Prepare and bake the oatmeal raisin bread. While it is in the oven, shape the chocolate cookies into balls and put them in the refrigerator. Just when the oatmeal raisin bread comes out of the oven, the whole wheat bread should be ready to go in. While it's baking, you can clean up the kitchen.

5. When the whole wheat bread comes out, put in the chocolate cookies.

Banana Chocolate Chip Mega Muffins

Makes 12 muffins

These are top-banana muffins and are excellent headliners for an afternoon snack. You can make them without the chocolate chips if you want to serve them for breakfast, or have the kids present to you a two-page brief on why the judicious consumption of sweets in the morning, said chips, should be tolerated.

1 ripe banana

½ cup low-fat buttermilk

1 cup sugar

2 eggs

1 cup semi-sweet chocolate chips

¼ cup vegetable oil

2 cups unbleached, all-purpose flour

1 tablespoon baking soda

1 pinch salt

1. Preheat the oven to 350°F. Lightly grease a muffin pan (spray oil works best for this) and then line it with muffin liners, decorated with your kids favorite characters, if possible.

2. In a mixing bowl, mash the banana with a fork until it is mushy. If the kids help with this, you might want to use a potato masher. Stir in the buttermilk, sugar, eggs, chocolate chips, and oil using a wooden spoon.

3. In another bowl, whisk together the all-purpose flour, baking soda, and salt.

4. Add the dry ingredients to the banana/buttermilk mixture and stir until just combined. Do not overstir or the muffins will come out lumpy.

5. Spoon the batter into the muffin liners so that they are ¾ full. You should have enough for 12 muffins.

6. Bake on the center rack for about 18 minutes, or until a toothpick inserted into the center of the muffins comes out clean or with just a few crumbs attached, although not smeared.

7. Let the pans cool on a wire rack for 20 minutes before removing the muffins.

Whole Wheat Bread

Makes two 5x10-inch loaves

Bread is magic. It's one of the greatest creations in the history of civilization, including zip-lock bags. Examine the flour, the oil, and the yeast. By themselves, they are basically inedible. Combined with water and baked, they are transformed into the staff of life. This is a basic whole wheat loaf with a little oatmeal added for texture, and it's the perfect way to introduce the kids to making bread.

½ cup warm water

2 packages dried yeast

½ teaspoon sugar

3 cups milk

¼ cup vegetable oil

¼ cup honey

1 tablespoon salt

1 cup unbleached, all-purpose flour

1 cup quick-cooking oats

5 to 6 cups whole wheat flour

TIPS

Yeast is a living organism and needs to be treated delicately. It only likes lukewarm water. If the water is too hot, the yeast dies; if it is too cold, it won't activate.

Kneading is a skill that's hard to describe, but once you've done it a few times, you'll easily get the hang of it. The basic steps are push, fold, and turn. With the palms of both hands, *push* the dough both down into the work surface and away from you. This flattens the dough slightly. Fold it back into a roundish loaf, give it a quarter *turn*, and push again.

1. Pour the warm water into a large mixing bowl. Stir in the sugar and then sprinkle on the yeast. Let this mixture sit for 5 minutes until it starts bubbling on the surface and smelling yeasty. This process is called proofing. While the yeast is proofing, combine the milk, oil, honey, and salt in a small saucepan and place on low heat. When the mixture is just lukewarm, remove it from the heat.

2. Stir the milk mixture into the yeast. Add the all-purpose flour and the oats and stir together. Add 4 cups of the whole wheat flour and stir assertively with a wooden spoon, adding more flour until the dough is smooth and not sticky. You probably will have to use your hands to get all the flour incorporated into the dough. The kids can start this process, but as more flour is added, the stirring gets tough and you're going to have to do a little Jack LaLane to finish it off.

3. Sprinkle some flour on your counter and dump out the dough. Knead the dough for about 8 minutes until it is smooth and elastic. You can break off chunks for the kids to knead and incorporate them back into the big dough later.

4. Lightly oil a large mixing bowl, place the dough inside, and then turn it over. This will give the top a light coating of oil so that it won't dry out as it rises. Cover the bowl with a dry dish towel and put it in a warm, draft-free place to rise for about 1¼ hours, or until it doubles in size.

5. After the dough doubles, pound it down in the bowl. The kids should like this. After the dough has been pummeled, divide it in half. Lightly oil two 5×10-inch loaf pans. Shape each half of the dough into a rectangle the length of the loaf pans and place them inside. Cover the pans with a dish towel and place them in the same warm, draft-free spot. Let the loaves rise until they double in size, although this time it should take only about 35 to 45 minutes. While the loaves are rising, make sure that the oven is preheating at 350°F.

6. When the loaves have doubled, place them on the center rack of the oven and bake for 45 minutes. A toothpick inserted into the center should come out clean when they are done.

7. Let the loaves cool in the pans on a wire rack for 30 minutes before removing them. Let them cool another 30 minutes outside the pans before slicing.

Note

The best way to store your homemade bread is unsliced in a brown paper bag on the counter. Plastic changes the texture, and keeping it in the refrigerator dries it out. If you want to freeze one of the loaves, let it cool completely, slice it, and put it in two plastic bags. Take out the number of slices you need and let them defrost at room temperature or throw them directly in the toaster.

Music

As a kid, I wore out Harry Belafonte's first two albums. No reason the current generation won't dig the original "Day-O" as much as I did. My kids are big fans of Burl Ives, The Chenniele Sisters, Chuck Berry, and The Coasters, so I recommend those as well. Original cast recordings of *West Side Story*, *Damn Yankees*, and *Guys and Dolls* are also big favorites at our house, so check them out as well.

Chocolate Cookies

Makes about 4 dozen cookies

These round, golf ball-sized cookies are one of my kids' favorites. They're easy to make, but they require an hour to chill in the refrigerator, so keep that in mind.

4 ounces bittersweet chocolate

6 tablespoons butter

1 cup granulated sugar

1 teaspoon vanilla extract

1½ teaspoons baking powder

¼ cup unsweetened cocoa powder

1 pinch salt

2 eggs

1⅓ cups unbleached, all-purpose flour

4 ounces (⅔ cup) semisweet chocolate chips

1 cup confectioner's sugar

1. Place the bittersweet chocolate and the butter in the top of a double boiler over medium heat. When they are melted, stir in the granulated sugar, mixing it in well with a wooden spoon. Then remove the mixture from the heat to let it cool for a few minutes.

2. While the chocolate is cooling, in a separate bowl, use a whisk to mix together the flour, baking powder, cocoa, and salt until they are well combined.

3. Add the eggs and vanilla to the slightly cooled chocolate mixture and stir with the wooden spoon until it is mixed thoroughly. Then stir in the chocolate chips.

4. Stir the flour mixture into the chocolate mixture, half at a time, until it forms a stiff but pliable dough. Refrigerate the dough for at least one hour.

5. After the dough is chilled, you're ready to make the cookies. Preheat the oven to 350°F. Lightly grease two cookie sheets (spray oil works well here). Measure the confectioner's sugar into a medium mixing bowl.

6. Break off chunks of dough and roll them into balls the size of golf balls—about 1½ inches across. Roll the balls in the confectioner's sugar and then place them 2 inches apart on the cookie sheet. Bake on the center rack for 10 minutes. They'll come out of the oven soft but will harden up as they cool. Let them sit on the tray for 10 minutes before carefully transferring them to a cooling rack. Then let them cool 10 minutes more before eating.

Oatmeal Raisin Bread

Makes 1 loaf

A "quick bread" that uses baking powder instead of yeast, this is great for breakfast, cut into thick slices and spread with butter and jam.

1½ **cups all-purpose, unbleached flour**

1 **cup rolled oats**

½ **cup whole wheat flour**

1 **teaspoon baking powder**

½ **teaspoon baking soda**

½ **teaspoon salt**

2 **tablespoons sugar**

¼ **cup molasses**

1¼ **cups buttermilk**

¾ **cup raisins**

1. Preheat the oven to 350°F. Lightly grease a 9x5-inch loaf pan with vegetable oil. In a large bowl, combine the dry ingredients and stir with a whisk until they are well combined.

2. In a medium bowl, stir together the buttermilk, molasses, and raisins. Pour the wet ingredients into the dry and stir with a wooden spoon until just combined. Transfer the batter to the loaf pan and let it sit for 20 minutes. Place the loaf pan on the center rack of the oven and bake for about 55 minutes, or until a toothpick inserted into the center comes out clean. Let the bread cool in the pan for 20 minutes before removing it and then let it cool another 20 minutes on a cooling rack.

Cookies and Milk

Of all snacks, this one is the ne plus ultra. Not because of its exalted culinary stature. Cookies don't compare to elegant pastries or delicate layer cakes. But what cookies and milk have going for them is that they speak of home, of kitchens with Formica tables, linoleum floors, and avocado-hued appliances. Cookies on their own are fine, but with milk they become something else altogether. The combo creates a synergy larger than its parts. Because a cookie you can gobble on the go or eat unconciously while watching television. But a cookie *and* milk requires attention. And time. It demands sitting at a table, using both hands, indulging in a ritual at once childlike and profound. Dipping the cookie into the glass, ideally with a Roy Rogers decal, certainly does much to help bring some peace to a troubled soul. Never mind "the road less traveled"; it's "the cookie less eaten" that is the source of so much of our contemporary anxiety and malaise.

Easy Dinner Party

Recipes make 12 servings

Twelve people are a lot to cook for. I won't sit here on my tuffet and try to convince you otherwise. But like the age-old epistemological question (is the glass of '82 Margaux half empty or half full), you can look at this undertaking in two ways. The half-empty approach is to forget it. Cook for 12? Hah! I'd be lost, trapped, my kitchen would become an M. C. Escher drawing. The half-full approach, which I am promoting, is that you just give it a shot, all the time repeating the mantra *I am cooking the same thing I would for four people, only in a larger pot.*

It only takes about an hour of savvy shopping and another hour or so of focused cooking to prepare this rustic yet elegant buffet for twelve. It's the kind of hearty, satisfying meal that will make you and your guests happy, which will cause them to drink more wine, which will make them even happier. This is the kind of party where you might want to get some serious charades going. Maybe distribute some disposable cameras for your friends so that they can document the festivities.

Another aspect of cooking dinner that should be mentioned is that because you're the one doing all the preparation, someone else (spouse? significant other?) should be responsible for the cleaning up—further motivation to get the invitations in the mail.

Menu

English Cucumber and Cherry Tomatoes
with Artichoke Tomato Dip
Mesclun Salad
Penne with Sausage and Eggplant
Sugar Snap Peas
Chocolate Pudding Cake

English Cucumber and Cherry Tomatoes with Artichoke Tonato Dip

Makes 12 appetizer servings

Vitello tonato is a traditional Italian dish in which slow-cooked veal is sliced thinly and served cold with a smooth tuna sauce. In this variation, the tuna, tonato in Italian, is enhanced by the addition of the artichokes.

One 6-ounce can solid white tuna packed in oil

One 4-ounce jar artichoke hearts in oil

½ clove fresh garlic

Cold water as needed

1 English cucumber, also known as *seedless* or *hothouse*

1 pint ripe cherry tomatoes

1 red pepper

1. Put the tuna and artichokes, along with their oil, in the container of a blender with the garlic. Puree until smooth but still thick—about the consistency of Mister Frostee ice cream. Add some cold water one tablespoon at a time if the mixture does not puree easily.

2. Rinse the cucumber and cherry tomatoes. Cut the cucumber at a slight angle into medium slices—about ½ inch wide. It is not necessary to peel the cucumber.

3. Cut the top off the red pepper and pull out the seeds and inner membrane, leaving the shell intact. Trim as little as necessary from the bottom so that the pepper will sit flat.

4. To serve, place the pepper in the center of a serving platter and fill with the tonato dip. Arrange the cucumber slices and cherry tomatoes decoratively around the pepper.

DRINKS

Wines

A light-bodied red wine would accompany this meal nicely. Perhaps a Beaujolais or an Australian Merlot, such as Rosemount, which has a lot of flavor for a medium-priced wine.

Mesclun Salad

Makes 12 servings

The secret to this salad is getting the mixture of baby greens known as mesclun. It's now widely available and usually comes prewashed so that all you really have to do is take the colorful assortment of greens out of the bag, arrange them on some salad plates, and drizzle on the dressing.

1 pound mesclun or mixed baby greens

For the dressing
6 tablespoons fresh lemon juice
2 tablespoons white wine vinegar
1/3 cup extra-virgin olive oil
Salt and pepper

1. Arrange the baby lettuces on individual salad plates or in a salad bowl.

2. Make the dressing by whisking the lemon juice and vinegar together until they are well combined. Continue whisking and slowly pour in the olive oil. Season with salt and pepper.

3. Drizzle a tablespoon of dressing over the individual salads or add to the bowl and toss.

Flower Power

You might have seen or heard about edible flowers that add an exotic and colorful accent to your salad. If there's a specialty food shop or hip green grocer nearby, they'll probably have some edible flowers, such as marigolds or nasturtiums, available during the summer. Two blossoms per person are sufficient to put some sparkle in the salad and start some conversation at the table. Oh, and they taste good, too.

Penne with Sausage and Eggplant

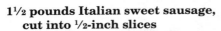

Makes 12 servings

Don't let the list of ingredients discourage you. This is not a very complex recipe to execute. It relies on the sausage infusing the sauce with its distinctive flavor, which is balanced by the eggplant and fennel.

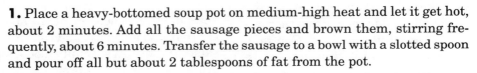

1½ pounds Italian sweet sausage, cut into ½-inch slices

1 pound Italian hot sausage, cut into ½-inch slices

1 eggplant, peeled and cut into approximately 1-inch pieces

6 tablespoons olive oil

1 large onion, finely chopped

1 fennel bulb, coarsely chopped

4 cloves garlic, minced

1 cup canned chicken broth

½ cup red wine

Three 28-ounce cans whole tomatoes

½ teaspoon dried thyme

2½ pound dried penne pasta

Salt and pepper

1. Place a heavy-bottomed soup pot on medium-high heat and let it get hot, about 2 minutes. Add all the sausage pieces and brown them, stirring frequently, about 6 minutes. Transfer the sausage to a bowl with a slotted spoon and pour off all but about 2 tablespoons of fat from the pot.

2. Return the pot to the heat and add the eggplant pieces. Cook them, stirring frequently, until they are lightly browned on all sides, about 5 minutes. Transfer the eggplant to the bowl with the sausage.

3. Add 2 tablespoons of the olive oil to the pot and spread it so that the bottom is glazed evenly. Add the onions and fennel and cook, stirring frequently, until they are soft, about 5 minutes. Add the garlic and cook 1 minute more.

4. Add the chicken broth and the wine and cook until the liquid is reduced by half, stirring frequently. Add the tomatoes, sausage, eggplant, and thyme and bring the mixture to a boil. Immediately reduce the heat to medium low and simmer the sauce, partially covered, for 45 minutes. Stir every 5 to 10 minutes to keep the sauce from scorching.

5. While the sauce is simmering, fill a pasta pot with cold water and bring it to a boil. When the water boils, add the remaining 4 tablespoons of olive oil and the penne pasta. Stir immediately to prevent sticking and a few more times before the water returns to a boil. Once it boils, cook the pasta for 8 to 10 minutes or until it is just a tiny bit crunchy in the center (*al dente*).

6. Season the sauce to taste with salt and pepper and serve. If you are storing the sauce, let it cool first. It will keep 2 to 3 days in the refrigerator or up to two months in the freezer packed in a well-sealed plastic container.

The Basic Rules of Charades

You might not have played charades since the last time you had a substitute teacher in high school, so here are the basic rules.

1. Divide the group into two teams and check for weapons. Have each person write down a clue, which can be the name of a book, movie, television show, play, or song. These should be collected by team, so that team A's clues will be used by team B and vice versa.

2. One team member picks a clue and stands in front of the group. He or she first identifies what category the clue is, using gestures to designate movie, book, play, and so on. He then has a designated amount of time (2 minutes is usually appropriate) to act out his clue to his team without speaking.

Tips

- Identify the number of words by holding up that many fingers.

- Hold the appropriate number of fingers up a second time to identify which word you want your team to guess.

- Place the appropriate number of fingers against your forearm to identify the number of syllables in the word you're currently working on.

- Pinch your earlobe if you're trying to act out a word that "sounds like" a word in your clue.

- Put your index finger and thumb close together to indicate that the word you're working on is a "small word," such as "the," "but," "as," "this," "it," and so on.

- Chop the air with a cutting motion if your team has the word but they need to shorten it.

- If your team is shouting out random answers and not getting what you're trying to do, point to your wrist and then your forehead to get them to "watch" and "think."

Sugar Snap Peas

Makes 12 servings as a side dish

Used to be these were one of the harbingers of summer. Sugar snaps are among the first vegetables to be harvested, in the Northeast anyway, and when they start appearing in the market, you know that soon you'll be setting up the sprinkler and donning your Hawaiian shirts because the serious part of summer is not far behind. However, sugar snaps are now available most of the year and although it's not as poetic, we might as well take advantage of it. Like snow peas, once the strings are zipped off, sugar snaps are eaten whole.

2 pounds sugar snap peas   **Salt and pepper**
2 tablespoons butter

1. Clean the sugar snaps by first rinsing them, and then snapping back the stem and peeling off the stringy filament that runs along the top of the pod.

2. Place a large frying pan with ½ inch of water on a high heat and bring the water to a boil. Add the sugar snaps and cook them until they turn bright green, about 2 minutes. Drain the sugar snaps in a colander, and then return them to the pan along with the butter. Toss the pods so that they are all lightly coated with butter. Season with salt and pepper. Serve immediately.

Music

Finding something to satisfy all 12 guests might be tricky, so go with something they probably are not very familiar with, but should be, such as *Yves Montand sings Jacques Prevert* or Stan Getz's lush and legendary album with strings, *Focus*. "Miles Davis Plus 19" playing the arrangements of Gil Evans would also be a mellow underscoring to this meal. If you were prescient enough to buy David McCallum's album when it first came out and savvy enough to hold on to it, definitely give it a spin on the hi-fi, if only to hear his version of Petula Clarke's hit "Downtown."

Chocolate Pudding Cake

Makes 12 servings

Meet Merlin the Magician with a plateful of this cake and you'll walk away with the trick for turning lead into gold in exchange for the recipe. This is it. One of those mysterious recipes that is incredibly easy, seems really weird when you're making it, but comes out transcendently perfect every time.

For the batter

2 cups unbleached, all-purpose
    flour

1½ cup sugar

¼ cup cocoa powder

4 teaspoons baking powder

1 teaspoon salt

1 cup milk

6 tablespoons butter at room
    temperature

2 teaspoons vanilla

For the topping

¾ cup brown sugar

½ cup sugar

6 tablespoons cocoa powder

2 cups lukewarm water

Note

The best way to serve the cake is to scoop out a section with a large serving spoon. Top the cake with a dollop of whipped cream and then spoon the syrupy pudding on the bottom of the pan over the cream.

1. Preheat the oven to 350°F. Generously butter a 9x12-inch lasagna pan (aluminum is okay). Measure all the ingredients for the batter into a large mixing bowl and beat with an electric mixer at medium speed or by hand with a whisk until well combined, about 1 minute. Be sure to scrape down the sides with a rubber spatula. Transfer the batter to the prepared pan and spread it out so that it evenly covers the bottom.

2. Put the brown sugar, sugar, and cocoa powder for the topping into a small mixing bowl and stir together with a whisk until they are well combined.

3. Pour the water over the batter in the pan, forming a pool on top. Distribute the brown sugar mixture evenly over the water. You now should have a wet, syrupy layer topping the batter. Carefully transfer the pan to the center rack of the oven and bake for 45 to 50 minutes, until a toothpick inserted halfway into the cake comes out clean. The top half of the cake should be crusty, while the bottom will remain somewhat loose. Let the cake cool for 30 minutes before serving.

A Casual Dinner Party

Recipes make 6 servings

In Manhattan we have the phenomenon of friends moving to the suburbs and, even though they're only 10 to 15 miles away (a not very strenuous bike ride), it's as if they've disappeared. Occasionally they return to the city because they need to get some real lox, they want to treat their parents to a Broadway show, or the kids want to see the dinosaurs in the Natural History Museum. Other than that, they stay confined in the land of wide supermarket aisles, double coupons, and drive-through dry cleaners.

Once a year, they might be lured from their lawns for dinner in the city. The first thing they comment on is the parking—how pathetic it is to keep a car in New York; how glorious it is to have a driveway. Then they start complaining about the noise and the *dirt*. You start to wonder, who *are* these pod people anyway? After all, only a few weeks ago, they lived here too. As a gag, I got some bullet hole decals to put on the windows.

To rankle them just a little, this dinner purposely has a homey feel to it to remind them that life in the harsh city is not completely devoid of comfort. And although it's a cinch to prepare, it doesn't seem like the kind of meal city folks have to throw together on the run.

MENU

Fatouche Salad
Marinated Flank Steak
Rice Pilaf
Honey Glazed Carrots
Apple Skillet Tart

Fatouche Salad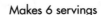

Makes 6 servings

Here I go, broadening your culinary horizons once again. This is a salad that uses more mint than you ever thought would go in a salad—that is, if you even had thoughts about salad and mint in the first place.

3 ripe tomatoes

1 seedless (English or hothouse) cucumber, rinsed and dried

1 head Romaine lettuce, washed and leaves torn into quarters

¼ pound Kalamata olives

½ cup fresh mint leaves, finely chopped

1 bunch curly parsley, finely chopped

¼ cup white wine vinegar

¼ cup fresh lemon juice

1 teaspoon curry powder

1 teaspoon salt

A dash of cayenne

¼ cup extra-virgin olive oil

drinks

Wine Selections

With dinner, serve a hearty French red, like a *Cotes du Rhone*. Rhone wines have a strong presence that will stand up to the meat. Look for the following in the $7 to $9 range:

Cotes du Rhone Belleruche (Chapoutier)

Cotes du Rhone "Moulines" (Duboeuf)

Cotes du Rhone "Parallele" (Jaboulet)

La Vieille Ferme "Reserve" (Perrin)

1. Cut the stems out of the tomatoes and slice them into 6 wedges. Cut each wedge across into thirds and transfer them to a salad bowl. Cut the cucumber in half lengthwise. Cut each half lengthwise into thirds. Cut each third into 1-inch pieces and transfer to the salad bowl along with the Romaine, olives, mint, and parsley.

2. In a small mixing bowl, whisk together the vinegar, lemon juice, curry, salt, and cayenne until well combined. Continue whisking and drizzle in the oil.

3. Just before serving, pour on the dressing and toss so that everything is lightly coated.

Marinated Flank Steak

Flank steak is an underrated cut of meat. Its rap is that it can be a bit tough. But marinating the meat will make it much more tender.

1 large whole flank steak, 2 to 3 pounds

1½ cups white wine

1 cup soy sauce

⅓ cup brown sugar

2 cloves garlic, mashed

2 tablespoons curry powder

2 tablespoons vegetable oil

1. Put the flank steak in a glass casserole just large enough to hold it. Mix the rest of the ingredients in a medium bowl until the sugar is dissolved. Pour all but 1 cup of the mixture over the steak, turn the steak over, and cover the casserole with plastic wrap. Refrigerate for 12 to 16 hours, turning the steak over at least once so that it marinates evenly.

2. Preheat the broiler. To cook, remove the steak from the marinade and pat it dry with paper towels. Place the steak on a broiler tray and broil 3 inches from the heat for 5 minutes. Turn the steak and broil 5 minutes more.

3. While the steak is broiling, heat the reserved cup of marinade in a medium saucepan over high heat until it begins to boil. Reduce the heat to medium and simmer the sauce, uncovered, until it is reduces slightly, about 2 minutes.

4. To serve, cut the steak widthwise into thin slices and spoon some of the sauce over the meat and rice.

Rice Pilaf

Makes 6 servings

Giving rice the pilaf treatment is an easy way to enhance its flavor.

2 tablespoons butter

2 shallots, finely chopped

8 ounces medium white mushrooms, thinly sliced

1½ cups white rice

3 cups canned chicken broth, or 3 cups water and 2 chicken bouillon cubes

½ teaspoon salt (omit if using bouillon)

1. Place a medium saucepan over a medium-high heat. Add the butter to the pan and as it starts sizzling, spread it so that it evenly glazes the bottom. Add the shallots, and mushrooms and cook, stirring continuously, until the mushrooms are soft, about 4 minutes. Add the rice and continue stirring so that the grains become slightly translucent and are coated with butter, about 3 minutes.

2. Add the chicken broth and salt, or water and bouillon cubes, and bring to a boil. Reduce the heat to low and cover the pan. Cook the rice until it is just cooked through, about 18 minutes. Fluff the pilaf with a fork just before serving.

Honey Glazed Carrots

Makes 6 servings

Using the peeled baby carrots now widely available makes preparation a snap.

1 pound peeled baby carrots
2 tablespoons honey

2 tablespoons orange juice
1 tablespoon butter

1. Place the carrots in a medium saucepan along with ½ inch of water. Bring the water to a boil, reduce the heat to low, cover the pan, and simmer the carrots until they are just cooked through, about 10 minutes.

2. Drain the water from the pan and add the honey, orange juice, and butter. Stir the carrots so that they are coated with the honey mixture and cook until the glaze thickens slightly, about 3 minutes. Turn off the heat and keep the carrots covered until you're ready to serve them.

Music

Something funky is in order for this meal. A solid urban beat to remind you guests how placid they've become in the burbs. Try the greatest hits of Parliment, James Brown, War, or late Temptations.

Apple Skillet Tart

Makes 6 to 8 servings

This is a rustic version of the classic French dessert "tart Tatin." It's one of those upside-down affairs, where the apples cook underneath the pastry. It requires a deft maneuver to flip over the pan, but you're a dad—you can handle it.

For the pastry
1¼ cup flour
¼ cup sugar
½ cup (1 stick) butter
¼ cup ice water

For the apples
5 tart apples, such as Granny Smith or Gala, peeled
2 tablespoons butter
¼ cup sugar

1 cup chopped pecans or walnuts

1. Preheat the oven to 350°F. Measure the flour and sugar into the bowl of a food processor and pulse twice to combine. Cut the stick of butter in half lengthwise and then into 2-inch pieces and add them to the bowl. Pulse 5 or 6 times, until the butter is the size of little peas. Add the ice water and process until the dough forms into a smooth ball, about 30 seconds. Remove the dough, wrap it in plastic wrap, and refrigerate until you're ready to use it.

Note

If you don't have a food processor, break the butter into little pieces with the tips of your fingers. Use a fork to stir in the ice water, then finish forming the dough into a ball with your hands. Work as quickly as you can, so the heat from your hands doesn't melt the butter.

2. Slice the apples lengthwise into quarters. Cut each quarter into 3 slices. Place a 10-inch, cast-iron skillet over medium-high heat. Add the butter to the pan and, as it starts sizzling, spread it so that it evenly glazes the bottom. Add the apples and pecans and cook, stirring frequently, until they are heated through, about 2 minutes. Turn off the heat. Sprinkle on the sugar and arrange the apple slices so that they evenly cover the bottom of the skillet and turn off the heat.

3. Remove the dough from the refrigerator and place it in the center of a 12-inch piece of wax paper. Place another piece of wax paper over the dough and roll it out with a rolling pin into a 10-inch circle. Remove the top piece of wax paper and flip the crust over onto the apples in the skillet. Peel away the second piece of wax paper.

4. Bake the tart on the center rack of the oven until the pastry begins to turn a light brown, about 30 minutes. Remove the skillet from the oven and let it cool for 5 minutes. Place a round platter slightly larger than the skillet over the top of the skillet. Using pot holders, grip the platter and skillet together and flip it over. It's best to do this in one swift motion with the skillet moving away from you. Place the platter on the counter and lift off the skillet, being careful of any escaping steam. Serve the tart warm with whipped cream if desired.

Martinis

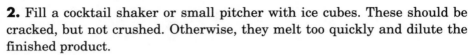

Makes 2 servings

When your suburban friends first arrive, remind them of their roots by offering them that most cosmopolitan of cocktails—a martini. Only one, of course, because they have to drive home, as opposed, say, to taking a cab. Here is the proper way to build two drinks at a time.

3 ounces vodka or gin   **Lemon peel**
½ ounce vermouth

1. Place 4 martini glasses in the freezer for a half hour or so.

2. Fill a cocktail shaker or small pitcher with ice cubes. These should be cracked, but not crushed. Otherwise, they melt too quickly and dilute the finished product.

3. Quickly pour in 3 ounces dry gin or vodka and a whisper more than ½ ounce vermouth. Stir 8 to 10 revolutions or shake for 5 seconds. Strain immediately into two frosted glasses and serve with a twist of lemon peel. Repeat for the remaining two drinks.

Ratfink

A popular party game in the fifties, it has since gone out of fashion.
The rules are simple, the results uproarious—at least for the first half hour.

Here's how you play:

1. Have your 8 guests sit in a circle on the floor. Those who haven't sat on the floor in several years might think this experience is enough adventure for one night.

2. Place 7 spoons in the center of the circle. There is no metaphysical reason why you use spoons other than that it's best once the game gets heated that there are no sharp objects around.

3. Take a deck of cards and separate the 4 suits for 8 different cards. Shuffle these 32 cards and deal them out.

4. The object now is to get 4 of a kind in your hand. The way you do this is by having each player, on the count of 3, pass one card face down to the person sitting to his right (or to his left if you live west of the Mississippi).

5. Once a player has all 4 suits of one card in his hand, he surreptitiously picks up one of the spoons. It's now up to all the other players to grab a spoon as quickly as they can. The one left without a spoon gets an "R." Lose a second time, and you get an "A" to go with your "R". The first person to spell "Ratfink" loses.

6. BUT, there is one little catch. The person who picks up the first spoon does not have to show his cards. Therefore, he could be bluffing. Another person in the circle can challenge him by saying, "I challenge you, you putz," at which point the person must show his cards. If he was bluffing, the bluffer gets 2 letters. If there was no bluff, the challenger gets 2 letters.

7. There should be a clever and somewhat tribal punishment prepared for the loser just to make the game interesting: going through the oven; singing an Al Green song; telling a deep, dark secret; or putting on a bra or underwear that's been in the freezer for a half hour. Make sure that you have a Polaroid camera around.

Faster Than Take-Out Dinner

Recipes make 8 servings

Leading pizza chains advertise 22-minute delivery. Factor in the time it takes to dial the phone, decide that you don't want any of the specials, find money to pay the delivery guy, figure out how much to tip him, and it's more like a half hour easy. You can make this dinner in less time.

The meals serves 8, which should feed your family plus a few extra guests, say a friend your kids invite for dinner, in-laws in town for an as-yet-undetermined reason, or your wife's nephew who's been staying in the attic and, though he hasn't found a job this year, will be certain to land one soon. As will his girlfriend.

These recipes aren't for a party *per se*. Instead, they are encouragement to turn an average dinner into an impromptu *fete*. Often those are the most fun. It's a great time to humiliate your kids by doing your Temptations impression. Or to tell them about the eerie coincidences between Lincoln's and Kennedy's assassinations. Or reminisce with friends about when every Beatles fan in the world thought Paul was dead.

MeNU

Green Bean and Peanut Salad
Hawaiian Chicken
Soba Noodles
Zucchini with Garlic
Fresh Pineapple and Malomars

Green Bean and Peanut Salad

Makes 8 servings

This salad features an Oriental dressing made livelier with the addition of the fresh lime. The flavor and texture of the peanuts give the green beans a surprising and refreshing taste.

1¼ pounds green beans
1 shallot, peeled and sliced
1 clove garlic, peeled and coarsely chopped
2 tablespoons fresh lime juice

2 tablespoons soy sauce
1 tablespoon vegetable oil
½ teaspoon brown sugar
½ cup unsalted peanuts, skins removed

Music

Something that sadly has gone out of style is for friends to sit around after dinner and listen to comedy albums. It's an activity reminiscent of radio days, when the family gathered around the radio for the evening's entertainment. Here are some classic comedy albums that would be appropriate to listen to after dinner:

The 2000 Year Old Man with Carl Reiner and Mel Brooks (also the two sequels)

Bill Cosby Is a Very Funny Fellow... Right?

How Can You Be in Two Places at Once, by the Firesign Theater (especially *Nick Danger—Third Eye*)

Woody Allen's comedy albums

Groucho at Carnegie Hall

An Evening with Mike Nichols and Elaine May

1. Clean the green beans by washing them well in cold water and trimming off the tips of both ends. Place the beans in a medium saucepan along with ½ inch of water. Bring the water to a boil, reduce the heat to low, cover the pan, and simmer the beans until they are just cooked through, about 6 minutes. Use a slotted spoon to transfer the beans to a bowl of very cold water to stop the cooking. Drain the beans in a colander and set aside.

2. Place the shallot, garlic, lime juice, soy sauce, vegetable oil, and brown sugar in the a blender and puree until the mixture is smooth, about 30 seconds. Add the peanuts and puree until the peanuts are broken up into small pieces, about 15 seconds. Don't worry if the peanut pieces are not of even size. Pour the peanut dressing over the green beans and toss well. Refrigerate until ready to serve.

Hawaiian Chicken

Makes 8 servings

This chicken is about as Hawaiian as Jack Lord, but that's what we call it at our house. You can call it anything you like. The addition of Chinese five spice powder gives it a slightly sweet and exotic flavor.

1 cup all-purpose, unbleached flour

3 tablespoons curry powder

8 skinless and boneless chicken breasts

2 eggs

4 tablespoons vegetable oil

¼ cup soy sauce

½ cup white wine

2 tablespoons brown sugar

2 tablespoons sesame oil

1 teaspoon Chinese five spice powder

1. Preheat the oven to 375°F. Measure the flour and curry powder into a pie plate and mix them together with a whisk until they are well combined. Beat the eggs in a small mixing bowl.

2. Dip a chicken breast in the egg and let the excess drain off. Lay the breast in the flour mixture, then turn it over so that it is completely coated with a light layer of flour. Transfer the floured breast to a platter and repeat with the remaining 7 breasts.

3. Heat 2 tablespoons of the vegetable oil in a large, heavy skillet over high heat until it is hot, about 1 minute, spreading the oil so that it evenly glazes the bottom. Add 4 of the breasts and cook them until they are golden brown, about 3 minutes. Turn and cook 3 minutes more. Transfer them to a 12x17-inch casserole dish. Wipe out the frying pan, add 2 more tablespoons of oil, and cook the remaining 4 breasts in the same manner.

4. In a small mixing bowl, whisk together the soy sauce, wine, sugar, sesame oil, and five spice powder until they are well combined. Pour the sauce over the chicken breasts and bake uncovered on the center rack of the oven for 16 to 18 minutes or until the breasts are cooked through. Serve each breast topped with some sauce. Reserve extra sauce for the soba noodles (see the next recipe).

Soba Noodles

Makes 8 servings

These Japanese noodles are made with buckwheat flour. They have a wheatier flavor than Italian pasta, which is made with semolina. Because they're made with a softer grain, soba noodles don't require as large a pot of water to cook in.

1 pound Japanese soba noodles

Note

Soba noodles cook very quickly, and they turn mushy if they are over-cooked. For this meal, you should drop the noodles in the boiling water just before taking the chicken out of the oven.

1. Bring a large saucepan of water to a boil. Once the water is boiling, drop in the soba noodles and immediately stir them with a fork to help prevent them from sticking. Boil for 3 to 4 minutes until the noodles are cooked through.

2. Drain the noodles in a colander and immediately arrange them on the dinner plates. Top with a few tablespoons of the sauce from the chicken (previous recipe).

Zucchini with Garlic

Makes 8 servings

Like Bud Abbot, zucchini, on its own, can be a bit bland. But throw in a Costello's-worth of garlic and it perks right up.

1½ **pounds zucchini, the thinnest you can find**

2 **tablespoons extra-virgin olive oil**

2 **cloves garlic, finely chopped**

Salt and pepper

1. Clean the zucchini by rinsing it well, drying it, and trimming off the stem ½ inch from the tip. Cut thinner zucchini (1½ inches across or less) into ½-inch rounds. Thicker zucchini first should be cut lengthwise in half and then into ½-inch pieces.

2. Heat the olive oil in a large, heavy frying pan until it is very hot, about 1½ minutes, spreading the oil so that it evenly glazes the bottom. Add the zucchini and cook, stirring continuously, until it is just cooked through and begins to brown slightly, about 5 minutes. Add the garlic and cook 1 minute more. Season with salt and pepper and serve.

Wine Selections
You'll probably want to serve a drinkable but reasonably priced white wine. Some Chardonnays in the $7 to $9 a bottle price range follow that should make you very happy. If your wine merchant doesn't have these specific bottles, he or she should be able to suggest something similar. If not, go somewhere else.

Columbia Crest (Washington State)
Glass Mountain (California)
Hogue Chardonnay (Washington State)
Kingston Estate "Riverland" (Australia)
R. H. Phillips "Barrel Cuvee" (California)
Rosemount Estate (Australia)

Fresh Pineapple and Malomars

Makes 8 servings

Nothing fancy here. Just the distinctively tangy taste of fresh pineapple accompanied by the best cookies ever made.

1 ripe pineapple   **16 or more Malomars**

Cut off the top of the pineapple, cut it lengthwise in half, and then cut it lengthwise again into quarters. Trim the triangular section of core from each piece and then use a paring knife to cut the meat from the skin. Discard the skin and cut the pineapple into 1-inch pieces. Serve these on a plate with the cookies.

Fun and Games

Youngsters today might not be aware that for several years Paul McCartney of the Beatles was actually dead. John might have said he was more famous than Jesus, but Paul was the only one to actually pull off the trick of coming back to life. Here are some of the clues from which we knew for certain that Paul could no longer be counted among the living left-handed guitar players.

On the *Sergeant Pepper* Album
His back was to us while the other Beatles were facing us.

There was a hand ominously emerging from the crowd that hovered right above his head.

The patch on his uniform read *OPD*, which did *not* stand for *Ontario Police Department*, as the nonbelievers insisted, but for *Officially Pronounced Dead*.

On *Magical Mystery Tour*
You can plainly hear the words "I buried Paul," on "Strawberry Fields," especially if you play it on 45 rpm.

The walrus is a Tibetan symbol for death, or so someone said.

Paul is sporting a black carnation.

On *The White Album*
The lyric "Here's another clue for you all/The walrus was Paul."

On *Abbey Road*
The license plate on the Volkswagen reads "28-IF"— the age Paul would have been had he lived.

Paul is the only one barefoot crossing the street. He's also out of step.

If you connect the dots on the wall, it says "3 Beatles."

Fast Fish

Friends are coming for dinner and maybe they don't eat meat. But before you start trying to figure out how to make nut burgers or tofu lasagna, find out if they'll eat fish. If they're health conscious, they probably do, because they know that fish is low in fat and high in omega-three fatty acids, which seem to be very beneficial to the health of one's blood. And by all accounts, healthy blood is a very good thing indeed.

But unless you grew up near a harbor, there's a good chance that you have some trepidation about cooking fish. You might be concerned that you have to actually clean the fish, ripping out distended guts and gills and losing your appetite in the process. Or perhaps you're worried that there is no margin for error when cooking fish, that if even one synapse segues slightly, in the direction, say, of a 3–2 count in the bottom of the ninth being announced on the radio, or a particularly lush Stan Getz cadenza playing on the stereo, the meal would be ruined. Or maybe you feel that it's not easy to give fish flavor—that it's too big a culinary obstacle for you to overcome.

This recipe anticipates all these fears and puts them to rest. You're dealing with fillets, here—so no cleaning, no bones, no fuss. They are simple to cook, and unless you allow yourself to become completely distracted with handicapping the feature race and forget the fish is in the pan, it'll be very hard to mess this up. Once cooked the fish needs only salt, pepper, and a squirt of lemon juice to perfectly flavor the fish.

So, Old Salt or not, after making this dish, you'll be the master of at least one way to cook fish and, hopefully, you will be spurred on to try some others.

MENU

Spinach and Shiitake Mushroom Salad
Fillet of Sole Canadian Style
Boiled New Potatoes with Dill
Steamed Asparagus
Frozen Yogurt with
Blueberry Peach Sauce

Spinach and Shiitake Mushroom Salad

Makes 6 servings

This salad is best if you use baby spinach leaves. They're easier to clean and have a milder taste.

10 ounces packaged spinach leaves, stems removed, or 1 pound baby spinach, stems removed

3 tablespoons vegetable oil

½ pound shiitake mushrooms

2 shallots, finely chopped

2 tablespoons water

2 tablespoons soy sauce

1 teaspoon sesame oil

Note

You can clean the spinach earlier in the day and store it in a plastic bag in the refrigerator. You also can cook the mushrooms up to 24 hours in advance. Reheat them in the microwave or in a small saucepan, adding a few more tablespoons of water and soy sauce to restore the sauce.

1. Rinse the spinach leaves well under cold running water to remove any grit. Dry in a salad spinner or pat dry with paper towels and set aside.

2. Heat the oil in a large, heavy skillet over medium-high heat until it is hot, about 1½ minutes, spreading the oil so that it evenly glazes the bottom. Add the mushrooms and cook, stirring often, until they are soft, about 6 minutes. Add the shallots and cook, stirring continuously, until they are soft as well, about 2 minutes more.

3. Add the water, soy sauce, and sesame oil and stir to coat the mushrooms. Turn off the heat.

4. Arrange the spinach on individual salad plates. Spoon the warm mushrooms and sauce over the spinach and serve.

Sole or Flounder Canadian Style

Makes 6 servings (6 fillets)

Using pancake batter might at first seem a disconcerting way to prepare fish. But ah, once you try it, seasoned only with fresh lemon, salt, and pepper, you'll be—dare I say it—hooked. "Complete" pancake mixes are the ones that require only water to be added.

1 cup "complete" pancake mix

1 cup milk

Six 4- to 6-ounce sole or flounder fillets

4 tablespoons vegetable oil

2 tablespoons butter

2 lemons, cut into 6 wedges

Salt and pepper to taste

1. Preheat the oven to 250°F. Measure the pancake mix into a pie plate and the milk into a shallow bowl. Dip a fish fillet in the milk and let the excess drain off. Lay each fillet in the pancake mixture and then turn it over and do the other side so that it is coated completely with a light layer of pancake mix. Transfer the floured fillets to a platter and set aside.

2. Place a large frying pan over medium-high heat. Pour 2 tablespoons of the vegetable oil in a pool in the center of the pan. Place 1 tablespoon of butter in the center of the oil. When the butter starts sizzling, spread it and the oil so they glaze the bottom of the pan. Lay 3 of the fillets in the pan and cook for 4 minutes, until they are lightly brown. Turn and cook 3 minutes more. Transfer the cooked fillets to an ovenproof platter and cover them lightly with aluminum. Place the platter in the oven, wipe out the frying pan, and return it to the heat. Repeat the process with the remaining 3 fillets and remaining oil and butter.

3. As soon as the last 3 fillets are cooked, season with salt and pepper and serve immediately, accompanied with a lemon wedge.

Boiled New Potatoes with Dill

Makes 6 servings

If you haven't had one in a while, you can forget just how good a not-overcooked boiled new potato can be, especially napped with a bit of butter and dill. It's subtle but satisfying and won't overpower the delicate flavor of the fish.

1½ pounds new potatoes, the smallest you can find

2 tablespoons butter

1 tablespoon chopped fresh dill

Salt and pepper

Note

Fresh potatoes should feel very hard. The surface should be smooth with no hint of sprouting and no bits of red skin flaking off.

Creamer potatoes, if you can find them, are the most flavorful potatoes I have tasted and are perfect for this recipe. A specialty grocer might stock them. Your grocer also might have baby purple potatoes; their flavor is not terribly distinctive, but their color livens up the plate.

1. Clean the potatoes by rinsing them under cold water, checking for any spots of dirt that should be wiped off. For decoration, if desired, use a vegetable peeler to peel a girdle of skin from the center of the potatoes, leaving the edges intact.

2. Place the potatoes in a medium saucepan with enough water to cover them and bring them to a boil over high heat. Immediately reduce the heat to medium and simmer the potatoes until they are just cooked through and a skewer goes in easily, about 12 to 15 minutes, depending on their size.

3. Drain the potatoes in a colander and transfer them to a serving bowl. Add the butter, dill, salt, and pepper and toss the potatoes gently. Serve immediately, although you can keep the potatoes warm for a few minutes by placing a plate or aluminum foil over the top of the bowl and setting them in the warm oven.

Steamed Asparagus

Makes 6 servings

Because it is being grown now in tropical countries, asparagus is plentiful and more easily available than ever before. Asparagus cooks very quickly and, depending on its thickness, requires only a few minutes in the pot. It's best served when it's still a tiny-bit crunchy in the center.

1¼ pounds medium asparagus   **Salt and pepper**
Fresh lemon juice

1. Clean the asparagus by rinsing it well in cold water and then trimming off the tougher section of the bottom—usually about ½ inch.

2. Place a large frying pan with ½ inch of water in it on a high heat and bring the water to a boil. Once the water is boiling, add the asparagus and cover the pan. Reduce the heat to medium and boil for 4 to 6 minutes until the asparagus is cooked through but is still a bit crunchy in the middle. Use your tongs or two wooden spoons to lift the asparagus to a serving platter or the individual dinner plates. Squeeze a little fresh lemon juice over them and season with salt and pepper. Serve immediately.

drinks

Wine Selections
This meal calls for a crisp, white wine served very cold. Maybe you should spring for a nice California Chardonnay, in the range of $12 to $15 a bottle. Or better yet, have one of the guests bring it. Any of the following would be quite suitable—
preferably, two bottles:

Franciscan *Oakville Estate*

Hess *Select*

Logan *Talbott*

Trefethen

Wilson Daniels

Vanilla Ice Cream with Blueberry Peach Sauce

Makes 6 servings

The best thing you could do to a bowl of vanilla ice cream is to give it to Linda Fiorentino and watch her eat it very slowly. The next best thing is to top it with this quick blueberry sauce.

1 tablespoon butter

3 tablespoons sugar

3 tablespoons fresh lemon juice (1 lemon)

1 pint fresh or frozen blueberries

1 ripe peach, cut into thin slices

2 pints vanilla ice cream or frozen yogurt

1. Place all the ingredients except for the ice cream or yogurt in a medium saucepan over medium heat and stir continuously until the mixture has thickened, 3 to 4 minutes (5 to 6 for frozen blueberries). Remove the sauce from the heat.

2. Place 2 hearty scoops of ice cream or yogurt in a decorative dessert glass or bowl. Spoon on the blueberry peach sauce over the ice cream and serve.

I see this as a quiet evening, with stimulating conversation—talking maybe about art, or foreign films, or the pros and cons of genetic engineering. The music should respect this mood. You probably *don't* want Sam the Sham and the Pharaohs or Steppenwolf. Try some Bill Evans—jazz pianist. The Brahms Trio for violin, cello, and piano. Heinz Holliger—oboist, playing Shumann. Mississippi John Hurt or Lonnie Johnson, both of whom sing soft, thoughtful blues.

Port

Port is a deep, richly flavored and slightly sweet dessert wine that has been made in Portugal since the 1700s. Up until the 1960s it was still made by men and women treading on the grapes in large stone tubs, bare feet being the perfect tool for pressing the grapes without crushing the pips. Aged first in casks and then for up to several decades in the bottle, Port is a luscious and satisfying way to finish off a meal. Fine vintage Ports can run between $40 and $50, with the most sought-after years costing hundreds of dollars. Very drinkable nonvintage Port, however can be found for $12 to $20 a bottle, and since you only have a small glass, it will last a long time.

Nonvintage Ports:
Chateau Reynella "Old Cave"

Fonseca "Bin 27"

Fonseca "10-year-old Tawny"

Warre's "Warrior"

Future In-Laws Descend for Dinner

Recipes make 6 servings

These would be the parents of your future son or daughter-in-law. So this meal is about making a good impression, reassuring these potential in-laws that their child is marrying into a solid, sensible family. (They don't have to meet Uncle Lefty until the wedding—that is, if his parole officer thinks it's a good idea.) This meal should be cozy and comforting—a reassuring menu that's sumptuous yet homey. It promotes the Good Life while still remaining thrifty and judicious. Just like your kid.

This meal also doesn't require too much work in the kitchen. It allows you to be present with your guests, exhibiting your wit, grace, and considerable charm. Also, with potential in-laws, because one of their objectives is to snoop around for any dirty linen, it's best not to let them out of your sight for too long.

Menu

Wild Mushroom Soup
Broccoli Sautéed with Garlic
Osso Buco
Bread Pudding

Wild Mushroom Soup

Makes 6 servings

Smooth and creamy, this looks like other mushroom soups but has a distinctly exotic flavor. Just in case they think you're being pretentious, you can inform your potential in-laws, "Oh yes, I frequently incorporate wild mushrooms into our domestic cuisine—sautéed portobellos on our burgers, dried porcini in our tomato sauce, and, if you do wind up giving the kids that car you promised them, you'll have to come back for some of my chicken and morels. (see page 214)."

2 tablespoons butter

¾ pound shiitake mushrooms, stems removed and sliced

¾ pound white mushrooms, stems trimmed and sliced

4 shallots, minced

¼ cup white wine or white vermouth

6 cups canned chicken broth

1 medium white potato, peeled and thinly sliced

½ cup half and half

Salt to taste

2 ounces enoki mushrooms and/or 6 chives for garnish

1. Place a heavy-bottomed soup pot on medium-high heat and add the butter. When it starts sizzling, spread it around the pan so that the bottom is glazed evenly.

2. Add the mushrooms and cook, stirring frequently, until they are soft, about 5 minutes. Add the minced shallots and cook, stirring, 2 minutes more.

3. Increase the heat to high and add the wine or vermouth and let it cook until reduced by half. Add the broth, bouillon, and potato and bring the liquid to a boil.

4. As soon as it boils, reduce the heat to medium low, cover, and let the soup simmer for 30 minutes.

5. Transfer the soup to a blender and puree in batches until smooth. Be sure not to fill the blender more than halfway with soup because it has a tendency to splatter, and you don't want to be splattered with hot soup.

6. After the soup is pureed, transfer it to a clean pot, add the half and half, and heat it gently over medium-low heat for a minute or two. Season with salt. Garnish with a few enoki mushroom and a couple of 2-inch batons of fresh chives.

Broccoli Sautéed with Garlic

Makes 6 servings

The addition of a hint of garlic perks up the broccoli just enough to give it a little zip.

1 head broccoli, cut into florets　　**2 cloves garlic, minced**
2 tablespoons olive oil　　**Salt and pepper to taste**

1. Cook the broccoli in 1 inch of boiling water in a covered saucepan for 4 to 5 minutes, until it is just cooked through but still a little crunchy. Drain the broccoli and lay it on a few sheets of paper toweling or a clean dishcloth to absorb the excess moisture.

2. Heat the olive oil in a large, heavy skillet over medium-high heat until it is very hot, about 1½ minutes, spreading the oil so that it evenly glazes the bottom. Add the garlic and cook, stirring continuously, until it just begins to brown, about 1 minute. You'll need to watch it carefully. Immediately add the broccoli and cook, stirring continuously, until it is heated through and the florets are all lightly coated with oil. Season with salt and pepper and serve.

MUSIC

Let the potential in-laws suggest what music to play during dinner. In fact, let them do most of the talking at dinner. Let *them* be the ones to reminisce about how they met, how she had to temper his profligate ways, how tough it was when they were first getting started. Those kinds of memories often lead to embarrassing squabbles and better their side than yours. It's a good idea *not* to show slides, but if you want retribution for years of your son or daughter not calling you on a regular basis, get out the photo album with the baby pictures. A few minutes with these will engender sufficient humiliation to make up for all the years your son or daughter stayed out late, dented the car, broke a vase, or neglected to clean up his or her room.

Osso Buco

Makes 6 servings

This is the classic Italian dish consisting of veal shanks cooked slowly in a rich tomato sauce until the meat is almost falling off the bone. It requires a little more than 2 hours of cooking time, so make sure you factor that into your dinner schedule. You might have to find a real butcher shop to secure the shanks, or speak to the butcher in your local supermarket a few days before the party and he or she may be able to order them for you. Also, this seems like a lot of meat, but much of the weight is in the bone.

1 cup unbleached, all-purpose flour

1 teaspoon salt

Freshly ground black pepper

12 sections of veal shanks (about 10 to 12 pounds) cut 2 inches thick

6 tablespoons olive oil

1 large onion, thinly sliced

1 celery stalk, thinly sliced

1 carrot, peeled and thinly sliced

6 cloves garlic, peeled and finely chopped

One 28-ounce can chopped tomatoes

2 tablespoons tomato paste

2 cups canned chicken broth

1/2 cup dry white wine

1. Preheat the oven to 350°F. Measure the flour into a pie plate and season with salt and pepper. Dip both sides of each veal shank into the flour and shake off any excess. Place the floured shanks on a platter.

2. Heat 2 tablespoons of olive oil in a large, heavy skillet until it is very hot, about 1½ minutes, spreading the oil so that it evenly glazes the bottom. Add the sliced onions, celery, and carrots and cook, stirring frequently, until they are soft, about 5 minutes. Add the garlic and cook 1 minute more. Transfer the vegetables to a 12x18-inch roasting pan.

3. Return the frying pan to the heat and add 2 additional tablespoons of olive oil and let it get very hot, about 1½ minutes, until the oil starts smoking. Immediately add as many shanks as will fit in the pan without touching and cook until they are brown, about 3 minutes. Turn and cook 3 minutes more. Transfer the browned shanks to the roasting pan, laying them right on top of the vegetables, and continue browning the remaining shanks. You will not need to add more than 1 tablespoon of olive oil to the pan for successive batches.

4. Add the tomatoes, tomato paste, chicken broth, and wine to the pan and stir together briefly, scraping up any bits of veal stuck to the bottom of the pan. Pour the mixture over the veal. Cover the pan with aluminum foil and bake on the center rack for 1½ hours. Remove the aluminum foil and bake 40 minutes more. Serve 2 shanks per person with the orzo (directions follow). Top both the shanks and the orzo generously with the tomato sauce in the pan.

For the orzo
1 pound orzo pasta

2 tablespoons olive oil
2 tablespoons extra-virgin olive oil

During the last 30 minutes of cooking the veal, boil a large pot of water for the orzo. When the water boils, add 2 tablespoons of olive oil and the orzo. Stir immediately to prevent sticking and a few more times before the water returns to a boil. Once it boils, cook the pasta for 8 to 10 minutes or until it is just a tiny bit crunchy in the center or *al dente*. Drain the orzo and toss with the extra-virgin olive oil.

Bread Pudding

Makes 10 servings

If these future in-laws need more evidence that your son or daughter comes from a thrifty home and knows the value of a dollar, then this dessert should do the trick. You use up leftover bread, for goodness sake. That says a lot. That you actually bought this challah specifically to be shredded for the pudding is none of their business. This also happens to be the best bread pudding you've ever tasted.

6 cups challah bread torn into 1-inch pieces (about ¾ large loaf)

4 cups milk

1 cup half and half

4 eggs

1 cup raisins

3 tablespoons melted butter

1 tablespoon vanilla

½ teaspoon cinnamon

1. Preheat oven to 350°F. Generously butter a 9½-inch tube pan. Place the challah pieces in a large mixing bowl and pour in 2 cups of milk. Stir so that all the pieces are soaked with milk and set aside.

2. Measure the rest of the ingredients in a medium bowl and whisk together briefly. Pour this over the bread pieces and stir with a wooden spoon until well combined. Carefully transfer the mixture to the prepared pan. Bake on the center rack for 1 hour or until the pudding is set and a toothpick inserted in the center comes out clean. Let the pudding cool for 30 minutes before serving.

Drink Selections

Wine with dinner makes sense here, what with everyone needing to loosen up a bit. A midpriced Italian Barbaresco or Chianti would be appropriate to serve with the osso buco.

If you want to make a kind of bravura statement after the meal, you could break out some of the superior cognac or armangac you keep on hand for special occasions such as this. If you don't keep them on hand, then you may not be aware of the velvety, smokey, luxurious flavor of these high-end spirits. Here are a few names to look for. They're expensive, but a little goes a long way. Hine "Rare and Delicate," Fussigny, Piere Ferand, Chateau de Fontpinot.

Instant Dinner

Recipes make 8 servings

There are many reasons why folks must drop in unexpectedly for dinner. Perhaps a friend's car broke down in front of your house and, seeing as it was dinner time, she rang your bell. Or the neighbors were heading out to a restaurant when they saw the apple pies cooling on your windowsill, so they stopped by to see what was up. But the real reason they might start coming by is because they know there will be good fixin's at your supper table and they're hoping to get an invite.

Once word gets around about your cooking skills, friends and neighbors are bound to show up unannounced—their kids, distant cousins, dogs in tow, clustered in the hallway, heads back, mouths open like baby chicks in their nest waiting to be fed. They'll even bring their own aluminum foil to wrap up the leftovers.

However, it's not every night you're preparing something that can be stretched to feed a few extra bodies. And suddenly the nice cozy dinner you planned for your family has turned into something else, something sinister, a kind of horror movie—*The Uninvited*.

That's why it's good to have an ace up your sleeve in the form of an instant dinner. Not only will it satisfy itinerant guests, but it's a great meal to have at the ready when you need to feed the family and you haven't done any food shopping for the last week and a half. This is a meal designed to be thrown together very quickly with what you're likely to have on hand in the fridge or the cupboard. If you are short an ingredient or two, send one of the guests out to get them. And tell them to buy some beer or wine too, whether you need it or not. This menu is more than satisfying on its own, but it easily can be enhanced with the addition of leftovers or other ingredients you find in your freezer or the pantry shelf.

MENU

Mushroom, Spinach, and Chickpea Soup

Carrot Salad

Pasta with Peas and Parmesan

Lemon Pie with Shortbread Crust

Mushroom, Spinach, and Chickpea Soup

Makes 8 servings

Served with some crusty French bread, this soup is a hearty way to start off the meal. No one would think you just whipped it up minutes before.

2 tablespoons olive oil

12 ounces mushrooms, sliced

1 medium onion, finely chopped

2 cloves garlic, finely chopped

One 10-ounce box frozen chopped spinach, cooked and drained

One 8-ounce cans chickpeas, drained

One 11-ounce can of corn, drained

One 28-ounce can crushed tomatoes

8 cups canned chicken broth, or water and 4 chicken bouillon cubes

½ cup grated Parmesan, preferably *Parmigiano-Reggiano*

Freshly ground black pepper

Note

You can add ¼ pound of chopped ham or any piece of leftover cooked meat to the soup—lamb or turkey cut into small pieces, for example.

1. Heat the olive oil in a soup pot over medium-high heat until it is hot, about 1½ minutes, spreading the oil so that it evenly glazes the bottom. Add the mushrooms and onion and cook, stirring frequently, until soft, about 6 minutes. Add the garlic and cook 2 minutes more, again stirring frequently.

2. Add the rest of the ingredients to the pot, increase the heat to high, and bring the liquid to a bowl, stirring carefully to make sure that the bouillon dissolves (if you are using it). When the liquid boils, reduce the heat to medium low and simmer, partially covered, for 20 minutes. Turn off the heat and stir in the grated Parmesan and fresh pepper to taste.

Carrot Salad

Makes 8 servings

It's hard to say what fresh greens you'll have in the bottom drawer of the fridge to put a salad together on short notice. If you just bought some Romaine and chicory, by all means, get out the spinner and whip together a salad of mixed greens. But you can't always rely on having the makings of a green salad on hand. I do notice that we usually have a bag or two of carrots in our refrigerator. This salad gives you a chance to use them all up.

2 pounds carrots, peeled

3 tablespoons olive oil

3 tablespoons fresh lemon juice

½ teaspoon salt

1 pinch of sugar

2 tablespoons fresh mint, finely chopped; or 1 teaspoon dried (optional)

1. Grate the carrots on the largest side of a hand grater or in a food processor fitted with the grating blade.

2. Transfer the grated carrots to a medium bowl and add the remaining ingredients. Toss well so that all the carrots are lightly coated with the dressing.

3. Refrigerate for at least 1 hour before serving. Serve on a bed of Boston lettuce if you have some or alone on a small, pretty plate.

Pasta with Peas and Parmesan

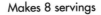

Makes 8 servings

This is a simple dish with a delicate flavor. There's nothing wrong with it as it is, but feel free to enhance it by adding a jar of artichokes, some pieces of cooked chicken, some diced ham, a few strips of bacon or sausages cut into small pieces, some diced roasted peppers, or even a can of flaked tuna. It's a chance for you to improvise using your now sharply honed culinary skills. In case you didn't realize it, this is the way recipes are born. Old women in 19th-century Tuscan kitchens create something new for their families' dinners, a big-time chef stops by on his yearly trip to gather authentic recipes, and a week later the same dish is twenty bucks at his New York restaurant.

4 tablespoons olive oil

1 medium onion, finely chopped

2 cloves garlic, finely chopped

1½ pounds dried pasta, such as penne, ziti, small shells, elbows, or bow ties

10 ounces frozen peas, cooked

2 tablespoons butter

½ cup grated Parmesan, preferably Parmigiano-Reggiano

Freshly ground pepper

¼ cup chopped fresh parsley

drinks

Wine Selections

Here's an opportunity to use up a few of those bottles of wine that have been sitting around for a while. If you have a choice, a hearty white wine would be best, like a California Chardonnay. By the way, if you need to chill the wine quickly, you can put it in the freezer. Just don't forget about it.

1. Place a large pot of water on the stove to boil for the pasta. While the water is boiling, heat 2 tablespoons of the olive oil in a large, heavy skillet over medium heat until it is hot, about 1 minute, spreading the oil so that it evenly glazes the bottom. Add the onion and cook, stirring often, until soft, about 8 minutes. Add the garlic and cook 2 minutes longer.

2. When the water boils, add the remaining 2 tablespoons of olive oil and pasta. Stir immediately to prevent sticking and a few more times before the water returns to a boil. When the water boils, cook the pasta for 8 to 10 minutes or until it is just a tiny bit crunchy in the center, *al dente*.

3. Drain the pasta and transfer it to a large bowl. Add the peas, the onion-garlic mixture, butter, Parmesan, parsley, and pepper. Toss the pasta until it is lightly coated and serve.

VARIATIONS

- Add 1½ cups cooked ham, chicken, or turkey cut into small pieces to the pan along with the garlic.

- Cut 6 strips of bacon into 1-inch pieces and cook them in the frying pan until they are crunchy. Remove the bacon and pour off all but 2 tablespoons of grease. Cook the onion in the remaining bacon fat and proceed with the recipe.

- Add two 6-ounce cans of flaked solid white tuna to the bowl just before tossing the pasta.

- Chop the fillets from a 2-ounce can of anchovies and add them to the frying pan along with the garlic.

- Chop 4 ounces marinated sun-dried tomatoes and add them to the pan along with the garlic. Use 2 tablespoons of the marinating oil in place of the 2 tablespoons of olive oil used when tossing the pasta.

- Add one finely chopped red bell pepper, fresh or roasted, to the pan along with the onions.

Lemon Pie with Shortbread Crust

Makes one 9-inch pie, 8 to 10 servings

Guests who just show up at your dinner table should, as a courtesy, bring some dessert with them. But then, given their unexpected arrival, courtesy is probably not their strong suit. You might have no choice but to dazzle them completely by whipping up a glorious dessert, such as this luscious tart lemon pie with a shortbread crust. Granted, not everyone has a shortbread crust hibernating in the cupboard, but because the ones sold in the supermarket last a long time, you might want to pick one up just in case.

3 eggs

1 cup sugar

½ cup plus 1 tablespoon freshly squeezed lemon juice

1 tablespoon grated lemon peel

¼ cup flour

One 9-inch store-bought shortbread crust

Note

The pie is best after being refrigerated for several hours.

1. Preheat the oven to 325°F. In a medium mixing bowl, use an electric mixer on medium speed or a whisk to beat the eggs and sugar until they are frothy and thicken slightly, about 3 minutes. Add the lemon juice and grated peel and continue beating until well combined, about 1 minute. Continue beating as you sprinkle on the flour. Mix until the flour is completely incorporated.

2. Pour the lemon mixture into the shortbread crust and bake on the center rack of the oven for about 40 minutes or until a toothpick inserted in the middle comes out clean. Let the pie cool completely before serving.

muSic

If you're pleased that these particular guests showed up without warning, then by all means grace them with some of your favorite tunes. But if this is the kind of behavior you want to discourage, then your music choice could help ensure that these particular guests will not return. As much of a fan as I am of his saxophone playing, any recording of Ornette Coleman on the violin will clear a room in a hurry. Some John Denver, Olivia Newton-John, or Captain and Teneil should also do the trick. And if they're still tapping their toes, anything by The Archies or Tommy Roe "Oh Sweet Pea, C'mon and Dance with Me" will soon send them packing.

Splendor In The Grass

Recipes make 8 servings

The perfect picnic, like a jazz performance, is a sublime example of controlled spontaneity. You want the standard picnic stuff to happen—kids picking wild flowers, first kisses, and longtime companions rediscovering their passion. You want kickball and scavenger hunts and a snooze in the shade. What you don't want is to run out of plates, forks, or drinks; or to have a shortage of sandwiches or to leave a vegetarian without any lunch at all.

You should have a cooler of some kind to keep the food cold. When choosing this, keep in mind how long a walk it is from the car to wherever you're making camp and make sure that you have the bodies to carry the cooler that distance. In some cases, it's better to divide the food into smaller, more manageable coolers that can be carried by the less burly among you.

Beer and wine can enhance a picnic, although some folks tend to conk out from the heat and fresh air. If you're one of these and feel that no one will mind if you nap for a while, by all means pack some up.

Menu

Rolled Smoked Turkey and
Cheddar Cheese Sandwiches

Tuna, Artichoke, Chickpea, and
Sun-Dried Tomato Salad

Oven-Roasted New Potatoes

Cucumber Salad

Lemonade

Blondies

Rolled Smoked Turkey and Cheddar Cheese Sandwiches

Makes 8 servings

A hoagy it ain't, but using flour tortillas here is a novel and satisfying variation on the good old sandwich. I usually make half with cranberry sauce and half with honey mustard.

Twelve 12-inch soft flour tortillas

4 ounces jarred cranberry sauce

4 ounces honey mustard

2 pounds smoked turkey, thinly sliced

1/2 pound sharp cheddar cheese, thinly sliced

12 large Romaine lettuce leaves, cleaned

1. Lay 6 of the tortillas on a clean counter. Working quickly, so that they don't dry out, lightly spread some cranberry sauce or honey mustard on the tortilla, and then cover it with a single, even layer of smoked turkey. Arrange 2 slices of cheese across the bottom third of the turkey and top with one of the lettuce leaves.

2. Roll up the tortilla and cut it on an angle into 3 sections. Place the sections seam side down in a plastic container. As you make a layer, cover it with plastic wrap. Repeat this process with the remaining 6 tortillas. Cover the container and refrigerate until you're ready to pack up the picnic.

Note

These sandwiches also taste great served in pita bread.

Tuna, Artichoke, Chickpea, and Sun-Dried Tomato Salad

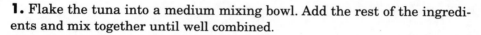

You can throw together this salad in a jiffy. It also should satisfy any guests at the picnic who don't eat red meat or poultry.

Two 6½-ounce cans solid white tuna, drained

Two 6-ounce jars artichoke hearts, drained and cut into quarters

One 12-ounce can chickpeas, drained

2 ounces sun-dried tomatoes in oil, chopped with the oil saved

3 scallions, chopped

¼ cup favorite bottled Italian dressing

¼ cup chopped fresh parsley

1 teaspoon dried basil or 2 tablespoons fresh basil

Salt and pepper to taste

1. Flake the tuna into a medium mixing bowl. Add the rest of the ingredients and mix together until well combined.

2. Keep the salad refrigerated until you're ready to pack the picnic.

Oven-Roasted New Potatoes

Makes 8 servings

3 pounds new potatoes, washed
   and cut in quarters with their
   skins on

¼ cup (½ stick) butter, melted

1 tablespoon dried rosemary

2 teaspoons garlic powder

2 teaspoons salt

Freshly ground pepper

Note

Do not store the potatoes tightly covered or they will get soggy. Put them in a container and cover them with a dish towel or paper towel. Pack them at the top of your picnic basket so that they won't get crushed.

1. Preheat the oven to 375°F. Put the potatoes in a single layer on a 12x18-inch baking pan and pour the melted butter over them. Stir the potatoes gently so that they are coated with butter and sprinkle on the rosemary, garlic powder, salt, and pepper.

2. Bake until they are cooked through and lightly brown, about 40 minutes. Let them cool before packing for the picnic.

Cucumber Salad

Makes 8 servings

A tangy, refreshing salad that's perfect for a picnic.

2 seedless (hothouse or English) cucumbers, rinsed and thinly sliced

½ red onion, thinly sliced

¼ cup white wine vinegar

2 tablespoons fresh lemon juice

2 tablespoons chopped fresh dill

1 teaspoon salt

1. Place the cucumber slices in a medium bowl. Add the rest of the ingredients and mix together until well combined.

2. Keep the salad refrigerated until you're ready to pack the picnic.

Picnic Essentials—A Checklist

☐ Plastic/paper plates

☐ Plastic forks, knives, and spoons

☐ Plastic/paper cups

☐ Napkins galore

☐ Corkscrew

☐ Sharp knife or jackknife

☐ Bottled water

☐ Sunscreen

☐ Blanket

☐ Insect repellent

☐ Balls and games

☐ Paper and pencils, for sketching, playing hangman, pressing leaves or flowers, and so on

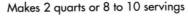

Lemonade

Makes 2 quarts or 8 to 10 servings

Pack this in a portable insulated jug with some ice. Be sure to prepare enough to fill the jug to the top because picnics tend to make people thirsty, especially if you get into some serious pillow-sack racing.

1 cup fresh lemon juice (10 to 12 lemons)

1 cup sugar

2 quarts water

Ice

1. Stir the lemon juice, sugar, and water together until the sugar dissolves, about 3 minutes.

2. Add the ice and refrigerate or pack in an insulated picnic jug.

Fun and Games

Pillow-Sack Race
Not recommended for adults unless you have a chiropractor in the family.

Rules
Put both legs in the pillow case. Hold onto the top with both hands. First one to jump to the finish line wins. Ten yards is about as far as the average human can get before collapsing.

Bocci
A simple game that can be played just about anywhere you have about 15 yards of semiflat open space.

Equipment
Two sets of four balls (softballs are the best, but tennis balls or baseballs will do)
One smaller ball, preferably one that doesn't bounce too much. Even a Wiffle ball will do.

Rules
Toss the smaller ball, called the *object ball*, away from you about 12 yards. Players alternate turns trying to roll their balls as close to the object ball as they can. The player whose ball is closest to the object ball at the end of the round wins.

Strategies
Try to knock an opponent's ball if it is close to the object ball or to protect a ball of your own from being knocked away by surrounding it with other balls of your own.

Blondies

Makes 25 squares

You'll be amazed at how quickly you can get these in the oven. They're great picnic fare. Perhaps not as traditional as apple pie, but a lot easier to transport.

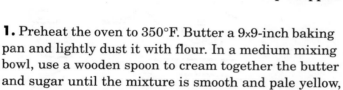

9 tablespoons (1 stick plus 1 tablespoon) butter at room temperature

1½ cups dark brown sugar

2 eggs

1½ teaspoons vanilla extract

1¼ cup unbleached, all-purpose flour

½ cup oats

1½ teaspoons baking powder

1½ cups (9 ounces) chocolate chips

¾ cup chopped walnuts

1. Preheat the oven to 350°F. Butter a 9x9-inch baking pan and lightly dust it with flour. In a medium mixing bowl, use a wooden spoon to cream together the butter and sugar until the mixture is smooth and pale yellow, about 2 minutes. Add the eggs and vanilla and continue beating until they are well combined.

2. In a separate mixing bowl, stir together the flour, oats, and baking powder with a whisk until they are well combined. Stir the flour mixture into the butter mixture until it is just combined. Stir in the chocolate chips and nuts.

3. Transfer the batter to the prepared baking pan and spread it so that it is in one even layer. Bake on the center rack of the oven for 22 minutes or until a toothpick inserted in the center comes out with flecks of cake but not smeared.

4. Let it cool for 30 minutes before cutting it into 25 squares.

Note

You can make blondies up to one month in advance. Keep them frozen in a well-sealed plastic container, although it might be difficult to not eat them all before the day of the picnic.

You also can make blondies by substituting half the chocolate chips with butterscotch chips.

Early Sixties Dinner

Recipes make 6 servings

If, like me, you're of the *I Spy; Mannix;* and *Wild, Wild West* generation, you probably have odd memories of the hybrid world of eccentric culinary creations that passed for gourmet food in the sixties. Hams covered in pineapple rings with maraschino cherries in the center, deviled eggs, Ritz cracker canapés, canned fruit kebobs, and Jell-O molds. It was a heady time.

But tucked away among the deviled carrots and fried celery with chicken livers were some classic dishes that I loved back then and still look forward to now. You owe it to your kids to revive some of those sixties classics and to your friends to make a meal to reminisce together about your favorite episodes of *My Mother the Car* and *T.H.E. Cat.*

MeNu

Greek Salad
Glazed Meat Loaf
Pureed Sweet Potatoes
Peas in Cream Sauce
Mocha Pudding

Greek Salad

While we were growing up, a Greek salad was about the most exotic food we ate in our house. The feta cheese, made from sheep's milk, made it seem like something from a National Geographic special had materialized in our dining room. The olives and sliced red onions were, for the most part, strangers to our table. For me, it was a harbinger of things to come—that there were all kinds of different cuisines out there, celebrating equally strange and enticing combinations of food. This salad also uses iceberg lettuce or, as it is augustly referred to in many parts of the country, head lettuce, which was the only lettuce we knew about back then.

¾ head iceberg or head lettuce, cut into 2-inch pieces

2 medium tomatoes, cored and cut lengthwise into eight wedges

1 cucumber, peeled and thinly sliced

½ pound Calamata olives

One 6-ounce jar marinated artichokes, drained

½ pound feta cheese, crumbled

½ medium red onion, peeled and very thinly sliced

6 hot pepperini (small hot green pickled peppers) (optional)

For dressing

¼ cup red wine vinegar

2 tablespoons fresh lemon juice

½ teaspoon Dijon mustard

⅓ cup extra-virgin olive oil

Salt and pepper

1. Wash the lettuce and transfer it to a salad bowl. Arrange the tomatoes and cucumbers around the edge of the bowl. Scatter the olives and artichokes around the center. Sprinkle the feta cheese over everything, and then top with the onion slices and optional pepperini.

2. Make the dressing by whisking the vinegar, lemon juice, and mustard together until they are well combined. Continue whisking and slowly pour in the olive oil. Season with salt and pepper.

3. Present the salad so that everyone can see how pretty it is, and then pour on the dressing and toss it well.

Glazed Meat Loaf

Makes 6 servings

I've eaten meat loaf just about my whole life. I can't say that about many other foods—even Scooter pies or the little shrimp cocktails my mom used to get in the collectable glasses. I stopped eating those unique concoctions long ago, but my palate continues to do a Larry Storch double take any time it's near a plate of meat loaf.

3 slices white or whole wheat
    bread, torn into 1-inch pieces

½ pound Calamata olive4 cup milk

1 green pepper, stemmed and
    seeded and cut into quarters

2 celery stalks, washed and cut
    into 2-inch pieces

½ medium onion, sliced

2 tablespoons butter

3 pounds lean ground sirloin or
    round

2 eggs

1 cup ketchup

1 teaspoon salt

1 pinch cayenne pepper

½ cup chili sauce

½ cup currant jelly

1. Preheat the oven to 350°F. Lightly grease an 11x4-inch loaf pan. Place the bread pieces in a large mixing bowl and pour the milk over them. Let the bread soak while you cook the vegetables.

2. Place the pepper, celery, and onion in the bowl of a food processor fitted with a metal blade and pulse until the vegetables are finely diced, about 15 pulses. If you don't have a food processor, finely chop the vegetables by hand. Place a large frying pan over high heat. Add the butter to the pan and, as it starts sizzling, spread it so that it evenly glazes the bottom. Add the diced vegetables and cook, stirring often, until they are soft, about 5 minutes. Transfer the vegetables to the bowl with the bread.

3. Add the ground meat, eggs, ketchup, salt, and pepper and stir the mixture together until it is well combined. Transfer the mixture to the loaf pan and smooth out the top. Bake on the center rack of the oven for 1½ hours. After putting the meat loaf in the oven, mix the chili sauce and jelly in a bowl. After 1 hour of baking, spread half the mixture over the top of the loaf. Bake 15 minutes more and spread on the remaining chili sauce mixture. Bake 15 minutes more. Let the meat loaf sit for 10 minutes before serving.

Pureed Sweet Potatoes

The perfect accompaniment to meat loaf. To serve this up right, you really need those dinner plates that are divided into three sections.

**4 pounds sweet potatoes, peeled
  and cut into 1-inch circles**

2 tablespoons butter

¼ cup warm milk

¼ cup real maple syrup

**¼ cup favorite bottled barbecue
  sauce**

1. Put the potatoes in a large pot and add enough cold water to cover them up to 1 inch. Bring the water to a boil over high heat, and then reduce the heat to medium and let the potatoes simmer gently until they are cooked through, about 25 minutes.

2. Drain the potatoes in a colander and transfer them to a medium mixing bowl. Add the rest of the ingredients and mash with a potato masher or an electric mixer on medium low speed until the potatoes are smooth. Serve immediately. If necessary, the sweet potatoes can be reheated in the microwave or in a low oven in a covered pan.

Peas in Cream Sauce

Makes 6 servings

I'll tell you right off the bat this is not a healthy way to eat peas. You're taking an essentially perfect food and adding fat—loads of fat—to it. But in equally good conscience, I can't present you with this sixties meal without an authentic vegetable concoction. Feel free to serve plain boiled peas, but if you want the Smithsonian interested in putting this dinner in an exhibit, you'd better go all the way.

1 tablespoon butter

1 small onion, chopped finely

12 ounces white mushrooms, thinly sliced

¾ cup heavy cream

1 tablespoon Worcestershire sauce

1 teaspoon sugar

1 teaspoon salt

½ teaspoon paprika

One 12-ounce package frozen peas, cooked and drained

1. Place a medium skillet on medium-high heat. Add the butter to the pan and, as it starts sizzling, spread it so that it evenly glazes the bottom.

2. Add the onions and mushrooms and cook, stirring frequently, until they are soft, about 10 minutes. Add the cream, Worcestershire sauce, sugar, and salt and bring the mixture to a boil, stirring frequently.

3. When the mixture boils, reduce the heat to low and simmer until the mixture thickens slightly, about 8 minutes. Stir in the cooked peas and mix until well combined. Serve hot.

Fun and Games

Twister is *de riguer* at a sixties party. You also could throw some old *Avengers* episodes into the VCR and ogle Emma Peel as you once did. At a well-stocked record store, you should be able to find a disc of classic TV theme songs, which you can play and sing along to. "And so it was planned he'd command... F-Troop!"

Mocha Pudding

Makes six ¾-cup servings

My favorite dessert as a kid was Junket, sort of a cross between Jell-O and pudding. But somehow, while I wasn't looking, Junket, along with professional baseball players who play for the fun of it, disappeared. My mom also made us chocolate pudding, which came in a close second. Her pudding came from a box. I don't think she knew it could be made otherwise. It wasn't her fault. Just good marketing. This pudding is superior to anything that starts out as a powder.

1 cup sugar

5 tablespoons unbleached, all-purpose flour

1 pinch salt

5 egg yolks

¾ cup decaf coffee

2⅔ cups half and half

1½ tablespoons butter

4 ounces unsweetened chocolate

1½ teaspoon vanilla

MUSIC

There's too much sixties music to start selecting. All of Motown, Muscle Shoals, the Mercy Beat, and Surfin' USA is all up for grabs. Pick your favorites and make a mix. Then, if you want to bring the era to its appropriate musical coda, put on Miles Davis's *Bitch's Brew*, Hendrix's *Are You Experienced*, or Zappa's *We're Only in It for the Money*.

1. In a medium mixing bowl, use a whisk to mix together the sugar, flour, and salt. Continue whisking and add the egg yolks, one at a time. Add the decaf coffee and stir until well combined.

2. Pour the mixture into the top of a double boiler. Add the remaining ingredients and cook over simmering water, whisking continuously, until the chocolate is melted. Cook until the pudding thickens, about 5 to 7 minutes.

3. Transfer the pudding to 6 coffee cups or dessert glasses and refrigerate until ready to serve.

drinks

Wine Selections

Boone's Farm apple wine or some Lake Niagara Chablis were popular wines back then, though those oeneophiles "in the know" drank only Almadén. The other wine rage of the sixties was Portuguese rosés, especially Matéus, in its quirky bottle. Tasted today, it's surprisingly refreshing. You might ask your wine merchant if he has other Portuguese wines. Of course, if you want the stopper-topped jug to make a lamp out of after dinner, you'll have to go with the Almadén.

Sleep-over Dinner

Recipes make 6 servings

Sleep-overs can be emotionally charged events for your kids, especially the first time a friend is staying over. Until this fateful night, your kids have been able to keep the eccentricities of your household under wraps. Flatulent fathers and mothers in pink rollers have remained cloaked in secrecy. But now they are going to see parts of your home that usually are hidden. With a scrutiny rivaling the IRS, everything in your home will be scrupulously judged, from the kind of spray flowing from your shower nozzle to the way you fold your towels. Sheets will be checked for frayed edges, toilets for the alacrity of their flush. You might have to put away any potentially incriminating artifacts—any cheesy magazines, your 8x10 publicity shot of Ursula Andress, your framed cover of Iron Butterfly's *In a Gadda-da-vida*. And Heaven forbid you should appear in front of one of your child's friends in your pajamas. It's bad enough that you exist in the first place, but to be waltzing around in your jammies would be humiliating.

Under especially intense observation will be the evening meal. It surely will be talked about in school—what you serve your kids, what strange or bland or downright inedible concoctions you force down their throats. In light of this pressure, I've designed a meal that is fun and funky and is not likely to alienate anyone. In fact, there's a good chance that one of their parents will be calling you soon for some recipes.

MENU

Ginger Carrot Soup
Garlic Mashed Potatoes
Barbecued Chicken Joes
Mock Boston Cream Pie

Ginger Carrot Soup

Makes 6 servings

My kids like this soup. It's got a touch of sweetness from the orange juice and just enough ginger to make it interesting but not so much that it enters into the realm of yucky.

1 tablespoon butter

1 pound carrots, peeled and cut into ½-inch rounds

1 medium onion, finely chopped

5 cups homemade (see the recipe for barbecued chicken joes) or canned chicken broth

1 cup orange juice, preferably fresh squeezed

1 tablespoon fresh ginger, finely chopped; or 1 teaspoon ground ginger

½ teaspoon curry powder

½ teaspoon salt

Chopped fresh mint for garnish

1. Place a soup pot over medium-high heat. Add the butter to the pan and, as it starts sizzling, spread it so that it evenly glazes the bottom. Add the carrots and onion and cook, stirring often, until they are soft, about 10 minutes.

2. Add the remaining ingredients and bring the liquid to a boil. Then reduce the heat to medium low and simmer the soup, partially covered, for 15 minutes or until the vegetables are cooked through.

3. Transfer half the soup to a blender and puree until smooth, about 45 seconds, being careful not to get splattered by the hot liquid. Pour it into a second pot and puree the remaining soup. Serve garnished with a pinch of chopped fresh mint.

Things *not* to ask your kid's friends:

1. So how much money does *your* father make?

2. Do your parents make you clean up *your* room?

3. Does your father talk in his sleep? And if so, has he mentioned any hot stocks?

4. Do you wear pajamas with feet in them like our little John/Jane?

Garlic Mashed Potatoes

Makes 6 servings

Can't go wrong here. On their own, these mashed potatoes are in everyone's pantheon of favorite side dishes. But add a hint of garlic and then spoon some of the barbecue sauce over them, and these potatoes become sublime.

3 pounds all-purpose potatoes, peeled and cut into ¼-inch slices

4 cloves garlic, unpeeled

¼ cup milk

2 tablespoons butter

½ teaspoon salt

1. Place the potatoes in a large pot and add enough cold water to cover them by an inch. Bring the water to a boil over high heat, and then reduce the heat to medium and simmer the potatoes for 20 minutes or until they are soft when poked with a knife.

2. While the potatoes are boiling, put the garlic cloves in a small saucepan with enough water to cover and bring them to a boil over high heat. Reduce the heat to low and simmer for 15 minutes. Drain the garlic and cut off the tip of each clove. Squeeze the garlic out of the skin into a blender. Add the milk and puree until the mixture is smooth.

3. When the potatoes are cooked, drain them in a colander and return them to the pot. Add the butter, salt, and the garlic mixture and mash the potatoes with a potato masher or an electric mixer on medium-low speed. Cover the pan until you're ready to serve.

Music

For me, it's Billy Joel. Put on any song by him and I cringe. I can't tell you why. I like some other pop music, but Mr. Joel sends me over the edge. Kids, once they're around 6th grade, develop these same kind of ferocious prejudices which, if you have children this age, you're probably very well aware of. And when it comes to music, there's no trying to second- guess them or open their minds to new sounds. Especially in front of their friends. So the best thing to do about the music for this party is to let your kids choose what they want to hear. Then you should sit there and enjoy it, regardless of how raucous or shrill it is. And whatever you do, make sure that you avoid the classic parent line, "You call this music? This isn't music; this is noise."

Barbecued Chicken Joes

Makes 6 servings

This is a distinctly fun and flavorful meal. Serve the chicken as you would sloppy joes, piled on an open hamburger bun. The mild barbecue flavor should win over most any guest.

One 7- to 8-pound oven stuffer roaster

2 tablespoons vegetable oil

1 medium onion, finely chopped

3 celery stalks, finely chopped

1 green bell pepper, stemmed, seeded, and finely chopped

3 scallion stalks, finely chopped

4 cloves garlic, minced

2 cups tomato puree

1 cup ketchup

2 tablespoons molasses

2 tablespoons chili powder

1 teaspoon Worcestershire sauce

1 teaspoon smoked hickory flavoring

1 teaspoon salt

1 dash Tabasco sauce

6 hamburger buns

1. Put the chicken in a large pot with enough water to cover it and bring to a boil over high heat. Reduce the heat to medium and simmer for 1 hour and 10 minutes or until it is just cooked through. Transfer the chicken to a large bowl to cool. Save the liquid by pouring it through a strainer lined with cheesecloth into another pot. Use it to make the Ginger Carrot soup or save it as chicken stock.

2. While the chicken is cooling, make the barbecue sauce. Heat the vegetable oil in a large, heavy skillet over medium-high heat until it is very hot, about 1½ minutes, spreading the oil so that it evenly glazes the bottom. Add the onions, celery, green peppers, and scallions and cook, stirring often, until they are soft, about 4 minutes. Add the garlic and cook 1 minute more. Add the remaining ingredients except for the hamburger buns and stir until well combined. When the sauce begins to boil, reduce the heat to medium, partially cover the pan, and simmer for 10 minutes.

3. Preheat the oven to 350°F. When the chicken is cool enough to handle, strip the meat from the bones and discard the skin. Cut the meat into thin slices and then chop coarsely.

Note

Chicken Joe can be prepared through step 3 up to 24 hours before. Keep refrigerated until ready to use. Stir in ½ cup of water before continuing with step 4.

4. Transfer the meat to an 8x16-inch casserole. Add the sauce and mix until all the chicken is coated. Cover the pan with aluminum foil and bake on the center rack for 20 minutes. Serve the barbecue over a hamburger bun the way you would sloppy joes.

Mock Boston Cream Pie

Makes 6 servings

This is not a true "mock" recipe, but ever since I was a kid and saw the "Mock Apple Pie" recipe on the Ritz Cracker box that used Ritz Crackers instead of apples, I've been entranced by the "mock." This recipe is every bit as good as most Boston cream pies, which itself is a kind of "mock" eclair.

For the custard
3 egg yolks
5 teaspoons cornstarch
¾ cup sugar
1½ cups milk
1½ teaspoons vanilla
1 tablespoon butter

To finish the "pies"
½ cup jarred fudge sauce
6 slices pound cake

1. Make the custard first. Put the egg yolks, cornstarch, and sugar in a medium saucepan and whisk them together until they are well combined. Add the milk, vanilla, and butter and whisk together.

2. Place the saucepan over medium heat and cook, whisking continuously, until the mixture bubbles and thickens, about 6 minutes. Use a rubber spatula to transfer the mixture to a mixing bowl. Place a piece of plastic wrap directly over the top of the custard and refrigerate until ready to serve.

3. To make the cream pies, first warm the fudge sauce in a microwave or in a small saucepan over low heat. Do not let it boil. Place a slice of pound cake on a dessert plate, cover it with 2 or 3 tablespoons of custard, and drizzle on a tablespoon of warm fudge sauce.

Chinese Buffet for Eight

Recipes make 8 servings

My Uncle Jack was the Chinatown aficionado in our family. Whenever we visited him in Manhattan, he'd take us downtown and lead us through the crowded winding streets to his special haunts. It was a unique and fascinating walk for a kid, past the store that sold live chickens, the tanks of frogs and turtles (where they take their last hops or strolls, respectively), the stands with the exotic vegetables, the apothecaries with the mysterious herbs and odd lizards floating in jars. He knew places off the beaten track, where the waiters actually said hello to him and showed him the highest tribute one can receive in Manhattan's Chinatown—not rushing him and his guests from the table when we finished.

Often we'd share a large table with some residents of Chinatown and witness strange and wonderfully exotic dishes arriving for the people across from us. These were a far cry from the suburban Chinese food I was used to—flaming Poo-Poo platters, shrimp in a lurid red sweet and sour sauce, and chicken with chunks of canned pineapple.

The food here for this dinner is relatively authentic, although the inclusion of asparagus is, I believe, a domestic variation. Start with the sesame noodles, which are prepared ahead of time, then serve the soup, the main course buffet, and dessert.

MENU

Cold Sesame Noodles
Shiitake Wonton Soup
Green Beans
Scallops and Asparagus with Black Bean Sauce
Chicken with Red Peppers and Snow Peas
Perfect Rice
Orange Slices

Cold Sesame Noodles

Makes 8 servings

These were made popular in New York about 20 years ago by the Empire Szechwan Restaurant on Upper Broadway. People would stand in long lines to get in to order the noodles. They're now a staple in almost every Chinese restaurant in the city, and for good reason.

12 ounces Chinese noodles or thin spaghetti

1 tablespoon vegetable oil

½ cup smooth "natural" peanut butter

¼ cup light soy sauce

¼ cup sherry or Chinese rice wine

1 tablespoon sesame oil

1 tablespoon fresh lemon juice

1 tablespoon brown sugar

1 garlic clove, coarsely chopped

1 tablespoon fresh ginger

Chopped scallion greens, for garnish

Note

Be sure to use non-hydrogenated peanut butter for this dish.

1. Fill a pasta pot with cold water and bring it to a boil. When the water boils, add the Chinese noodles or pasta. Stir immediately to prevent sticking and a few more times before the water returns to a boil. When it boils, cook the noodles for 3 to 4 minutes, or the pasta for 8 to 10 minutes, until they are completely cooked. Drain the noodles or pasta in a colander, shaking it well to release as much water as possible. Pour on the vegetable oil and toss so that the noodles are lightly coated and transfer them to a serving bowl.

2. While the water is boiling, place the remaining ingredients, except the scallions, in the bowl of a food processor fitted with a metal blade or a blender and process until smooth. Pour the sauce over the noodles and toss so that they are lightly coated. Garnish with the chopped scallions.

Wonton Soup with Wild Mushrooms

Makes 8 servings

Betcha didn't think when you were sitting in your treehouse hideaway, whispering into your Man from U.N.C.L.E. walkie-talkie ballpoint and loading the booby trap with caps on your James Bond briefcase that one day you'd be making your own wonton soup...from scratch. But here you are, calm as Napoleon Solo, wantonly making wontons in your kitchen.

2 quarts canned chicken broth

2 pounds chicken legs

1/2 pound shiitake mushrooms, stemmed (with the stems saved) and thinly sliced

1-inch piece ginger, peeled and thinly sliced

8 whole scallions, stems cut off

1 teaspoon salt

2 tablespoons vegetable oil

2 whole scallions, finely chopped

2 tablespoons brown sugar

2 teaspoons soy sauce

1 teaspoon sesame oil

25 wonton skins

1 egg, well beaten

One 12-ounce can baby corn

Chopped scallion greens for garnish

1 carrot, shredded, for garnish

1. To make a double-strength broth, put the chicken broth, chicken legs, shiitake stems, ginger, whole scallions, and salt into a soup pot and bring to a boil over high heat. When it boils, reduce the heat to medium low and simmer, partially covered, for 35 minutes, until the chicken is cooked through. Strain the soup through a colander into another pot and discard the solids or save the cooked chicken for another use. Use a large spoon to skim off the fat collected on the top of the broth.

> **Note**
>
> It's important not to let the wonton skins dry out before filling them. Once wontons are made however, it's okay to leave them on the counter.

2. While the broth is simmering, bring a large pot of water to a boil and assemble the wontons. Heat the oil in a medium, heavy skillet over high heat until it is very hot, about 1½ minutes, spreading the oil so that it evenly glazes the bottom. Add the shiitake mushroom caps and cook, stirring continuously, until they soften, about 5 minutes. Transfer the shiitakes to a cutting board and chop them finely. Place them in a bowl along with the chopped scallion, brown sugar, soy sauce, and sesame oil and mix together.

(recipe continues)

3. Lay a wonton skin on the counter. With a pastry brush or your finger, coat the skin with a very light layer of the beaten egg. Place a teaspoon of the mushroom mixture in the center of the skin and fold it into a triangle. Press down the edges and set the wonton on a platter. Repeat with the remaining skins.

4. Cook the wontons in the boiling water until they are soft, about 6 minutes. Arrange the soup bowls on the counter. Fill each halfway with broth. Add three wontons and a few baby corn. Garnish each bowl with a sprinkling of chopped scallions and shredded carrots.

Fun and Games

If there is a Chinatown near where you live, there's a good chance you can pick up some fortune cookies to distribute during dessert. If not, then you can make up your own fortunes and let the guests choose them after dinner. Have your kids help you write some original ones in addition to re-creating some of your favorites from meals past. I honestly got a fortune once that read, "Beware of bus drivers named George." Of course, as most of us know, the true meaning only emerges when you add the phrase "between the sheets" to the end of the fortune, as in "You will soon find exactly what you are looking for...*between the sheets.*" It even works with warnings about bus drivers named George.

Green Beans

Makes 8 servings

Quickly stir-fry these in a wok or frying pan.

1 pound green beans
1 tablespoon vegetable oil
2 tablespoons bottled teriyaki sauce

1. Clean the green beans by washing them under cold water and patting them dry with a towel. Trim the tips off each end of the bean.

2. Heat the oil in a wok or a large, heavy skillet over high heat until it is very hot, about 2 minutes, spreading the oil so that it evenly glazes the bottom. Add the green beans and cook, stirring continuously, until they are just cooked through, about 4 minutes. If they get a little brown on the outside, don't worry. Add the teriyaki sauce and cook 1 minute more, stirring continuously until all the beans are lightly coated. Serve immediately.

Scallops and Asparagus with Black Bean Sauce

Makes 8 servings

This is a serious dish, centered around the exotic flavor of fermented black beans. There are a lot of ingredients for this dish, but it goes together very quickly.

½ cup canned chicken broth, or 1 bouillon cube dissolved in ½ cup water

3 tablespoons soy sauce

2 tablespoons fermented black bean paste

2 tablespoons sherry or Chinese rice wine

2 tablespoons vegetable oil

¼ teaspoon red pepper flakes

6 cloves garlic, finely chopped

1-inch piece ginger, peeled and finely chopped

4 whole scallions, finely chopped

2½ pounds medium sea scallops

½ pound asparagus, ends trimmed and cut into 2-inch pieces

1. Preheat the oven to 450°F. You'll need a large, ovenproof frying pan with a cover. If you don't have a cover, make one out of aluminum foil. In a small bowl, mix together the chicken broth (or bouillon cube and water mixture), soy sauce, black bean paste, and sherry and set aside.

2. Heat the oil in a large, heavy skillet over high heat until it is very hot, about 2 minutes, spreading the oil so that it evenly glazes the bottom. Add the garlic, ginger, and scallions and cook for 1 minute, stirring continuously. Add the scallops and asparagus and cook 2 minutes more, stirring continuously.

3. Cover the pan and place it in the hot oven for 5 minutes. Carefully remove the pan and transfer the contents to a serving platter. Be sure to scrape out all the sauce in the bottom of the pan.

drinks

Since the 8th century, tea has been the traditional drink to have with dinner in China. Green tea is a most popular Chinese tea and can be found in specialty food stores or in an Oriental market. Green tea is an unfermented tea, giving it a slightly more bitter flavor than the black fermented teas.

Chicken with Ginger and Cashews

Makes 8 servings

One aspect of Chinese cuisine that I especially enjoy is the addition of nuts to the main dishes. This recipe combines cashews and chicken. If you can't find cashews, unsalted peanuts will do. Be sure to strip the reddish skin off the nuts before using them.

2 tablespoons rice wine

2 tablespoons soy sauce

2 tablespoons chicken broth

1 tablespoon brown sugar

2 teaspoons sesame oil

5 tablespoons vegetable oil

4 boneless chicken breasts, cut into ½-inch slivers

2 red peppers, cored, seeded and cut into ½-inch strips

¼ pound snow peas, stem and strings removed

3 scallions greens, cut into 1-inch pieces

1-inch piece ginger, peeled and finely chopped

½ cup roasted unsalted cashews

4 cloves garlic, minced

1. Mix the rice wine, soy sauce, chicken broth, brown sugar, and sesame oil in a small bowl until the sugar is dissolved. Set aside.

2. Heat the vegetable oil in a wok or large, heavy skillet over high heat until it is very hot, about 2 minutes, spreading the oil so that it evenly glazes the bottom. Add the chicken pieces and cook, stirring continuously, until they are cooked through, about 4 minutes. Transfer the chicken to a mixing bowl, wipe out the pan, and return it to the heat.

Note

You can prepare the recipe through step 3 before the guests arrive. You then can complete the dish while the Scallops and Asparagus recipe is in the oven.

3. Add the remaining 2 tablespoons of vegetable oil and let it get hot, about 1 minute. Add the pepper, snow peas, scallions, ginger, and cashews and cook, stirring continuously, until the peppers are soft on the outside but still crunchy inside, about 2 minutes. Add the garlic and cook 1 minute more, stirring continuously.

4. Return the chicken to the pan. Pour on the sauce and stir so that everything is lightly coated and the chicken is heated through, about 1 minute. Serve immediately.

Perfect Rice

Makes 8 servings

I once worked as a waiter in a summer camp. The rice they made always came out in a big gelatinous mess, like something Ed Wood would use as an alien special effect. The joke I made when serving these lumps the size of snowballs was, "Would you like one rice, or two?" You, however, won't be preparing rice like that because you know the secrets, which are to measure exactly, to not open the pot during cooking, to keep the heat low, and to fluff with a fork just before serving.

3½ cups water   **3 cups white or regular rice**
1 tablespoon butter

1. Bring the water and butter to a boil over high heat in a heavy-bottomed saucepan with a tight-fitting lid.

2. When the water boils, add the rice and stir once. When the liquid returns to a boil, immediately cover the pan and reduce the heat to low. Cook for 18 minutes without taking off the cover.

3. Remove from the heat. The rice can stay warm in the pan for 10 to 15 minutes before serving.

Note

Rice is best made just before serving—reheating it without ruining its texture is difficult.

Fresh Orange Slices

Makes 8 servings

Chinese cooking isn't big on desserts. Because they don't use a lot of dairy, it's hard to get what you need to make a chocolate eclair or filling for a canoli. And after three courses, fresh fruit is probably all anyone can handle.

6 naval oranges

Cut the orange lengthwise in half, and then cut each half lengthwise into thirds. Serve on a decorative platter.

Backyard Burger Ruckus

Recipes make 8 servings

The backyard was meant for the barbecue and the barbecue was meant for burgers. Regrettably, some folks are reluctant to eat hamburgers these days. Something about the fat and the cholesterol. But while this is true for other kinds of red meat, hamburgers have been granted a special immunity because they make everyone feel so good. But the catch is they have to be grilled at home and you have to eat them with your family with lots of ketchup and mustard. And they have to be followed by a game of catch or touch football along with a tree to climb and a hammock for Dad to rest in when his cooking duties are done. Still, many people refuse to believe that hamburgers are good for you. That's because their brains have been taken over by aliens. To appease them, so they don't get angry and send rays into the barbecue and douse the coals, I've included alternative "lighter" burgers made from turkey and swordfish. They should satisfy almost any guest even if his feet are webbed.

MeNu

Basic Burger
Swordfish Burger
Ragin' Cajun Turkey Burger
Sicilian Potato Salad
Grilled Zucchini
Apple Blueberry Crisp
Rum Punch

Basic Burgers

Makes 8 burgers

The burger is its own food group. Think of the nutrition pyramid: the burger is the sphinx nearby, majestic and inscrutable. And like the sphinx, a burger defies adornment; it needs to be embraced as is, a statement of the mysterious nature of the universe. Like a weekend in Venice, a burger is one of those few things in life you have to work hard at to screw up. Some say the fattier meat makes for juicier burgers, but 10 percent fat is sufficient fat. Any more and the charcoals flame up and start going all Carmen Miranda on you. The real secret to making juicy, luscious, drippingly succulent burgers is to have your fire nice and hot and not to cook them too long.

Bake me no Alaskas and flambé me no crepes. I pay homage to the noble burger, a down-home blues to Cordon's more effete Bleus. This is a perfect food. If you don't like them, to paraphrase The Bard, "The fault, Dear Reader, is not in the Burger, but in yourself."

3 pounds ground round or sirloin   **8 soft rolls or English muffins**

Note

Nestling your perfect burger in a packaged hamburger roll is like wrapping it in used Kleenex. If you're going to spend the time to make your burgers right, then go the distance and get some bakery rolls, soft egg twists, or Kaiser-style rolls. If there isn't a bakery near you or you've just entered the Witness Protection program and don't yet know your way around your new hometown, go with lightly toasted English muffins, especially the sourdough variety.

For charcoal grilling

1. Get the charcoal started. If you don't have a gas grill, you'll need some way to get the charcoals lit. I strongly suggest that you refrain from using the lighter-fluid method. It might be psychological, but I really feel that the fluid imparts a subtle flavor to the food that does not enhance its taste. If you must use fluid, follow the directions on the container, being sure to show the necessary patience required to allow the fluid to soak into the coals. In my opinion, the preferable way to get the coals lit is by using a chimney or an electric coil. The chimney method uses a metal cylinder that holds the coals and a few pages of newspaper to get them started. The coil is plugged in and heats up under the coals, heating them sufficiently after a few minutes. Both devices are readily available at any decent hardware store. Follow the accompanying instructions. I think you'll find them easier and ultimately more reliable than the fluid, and without any residual smell or taste.

2. While the coals are heating, shape the meat into burgers about 4 inches across and 1½ inches thick.

3. When the coals have ashed over, spread them evenly over the bottom of the grill. Place the burgers on the grill and cook them until the bottoms are nicely browned, about 5 minutes. Turn and cook about 4 minutes more for rare or about 5 minutes more for medium. For well done, you'll have to consult another cookbook.

Accessorizing Your Burger

Doyennes of fashion insist that accessories make *The Look*. Translated into burger terms, this means the burger itself is only an excuse to support the cheese, mushrooms, onions, or other toppings. I'm not a big fan of toppings. You can make your own decisions. Here are some options.

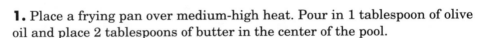

Mushrooms and Onions

Makes enough to top 8 burgers

1 tablespoon olive oil
2 tablespoons butter
1 large onion, sliced
12 ounces white mushrooms, sliced

Salt and freshly ground black pepper
Worcestershire sauce

1. Place a frying pan over medium-high heat. Pour in 1 tablespoon of olive oil and place 2 tablespoons of butter in the center of the pool.

2. When the butter stops sizzling, spread it around the pan so that the entire bottom is glazed and add the onion and mushrooms.

3. Cook, stirring frequently, until the onions are soft and the mushrooms release all their juice, about 7 minutes.

4. Season with salt, pepper, and a few teaspoons of Worcestershire sauce.

Portobello Mushrooms

Makes enough to top 8 burgers

2 tablespoons olive oil
2 shallots, finely chopped

12 ounces portobello mushrooms
Salt and freshly ground black pepper

1. Heat the olive oil in a large, heavy skillet until it is very hot, about 1½ minutes. During this time, spread the oil so that it evenly glazes the bottom.

2. Add the shallots and portobello mushrooms and cook, stirring often, until the mushrooms are cooked through, about 5 minutes.

3. Season with salt and pepper.

Touch football, Wiffle ball, badminton, and croquet are all great backyard fun. Just make sure that you don't throw any long passes into the barbecue. If there are a lot of little kids, you might try a game of tag. Just make sure that you have some oxygen on hand for the adults.

Knock Down

If you're keen on a game of Wiffle ball and you only have 5 or 6 people, you can play Knock Down. The rules are simple. Each player keeps track of his own score. Players take the field, one person pitching, one on first, another at shortstop, and the others placed strategically on the field. Each batter hits until he makes out. The defensive play is just like a real game—trying to throw the ball to first to get the batters out. If the batter hits safely, an "imaginary runner" marks his spot on the base paths and advances according to how the batter does. If the batter gets a double his first time up and a single the second time, for example, the imaginary runner on second moves to third. Once the batter makes out, he or she moves to the field to play in the outfield, the pitcher moves in to bat, the first baseman moves over to pitch, and the shortstop moves to first. When everyone has batted, you've played an inning. The game goes usually for 5 or 6 innings.

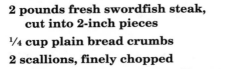

Swordfish Burgers

Makes 8 burgers

Swordfish is a meaty enough fish to hold together nicely in a burger shape. The touch of ginger gives it an added zest. Serve with honey mustard and some Boston lettuce on a soft roll, French bread, or English muffin. You will need a food processor to prepare this dish.

2 pounds fresh swordfish steak, cut into 2-inch pieces

¼ cup plain bread crumbs

2 scallions, finely chopped

2 tablespoons finely chopped fresh cilantro

1 tablespoon chopped fresh ginger

1 tablespoon soy sauce

1 tablespoon sherry

Salt and freshly ground black pepper

Note

If you don't have a hinged grill, clean the grill on your barbecue well and then brush it with oil before lighting the coals.

1. Place the swordfish in a food processor and process until it is smooth.

2. Transfer the swordfish to a mixing bowl, add the remaining ingredients, and mix together with your fingers until well combined. Shape the mixture into burgers that are 3 inches across and 1 inch high. Place them on a platter and put them in the refrigerator while you light the barbecue. You can make these burgers up to three hours before cooking.

3. Get the charcoal started. When the coals have ashed over, spread them evenly over the bottom of the grill. Place the swordfish burgers in a hinged grill and cook them until they are lightly brown on the bottom, about 7 minutes. Turn and cook them 6 minutes more. Serve on a soft roll with Boston lettuce and a bit of honey mustard.

Ragin' Cajun Turkey Burgers

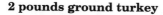
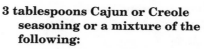

Makes 8 burgers

Turkey burgers are kind of bland on their own; the addition of the Cajun spices helps them out. Cooking these on the barbecue can be tricky because they tend to fall apart. Make sure that the grill is clean and lightly oiled before lighting the coals.

2 pounds ground turkey
1 egg
2 egg whites
1 small onion, grated
¼ cup bread crumbs

3 tablespoons Cajun or Creole seasoning or a mixture of the following:
  1 tablespoon chili powder
  2 teaspoons onion powder
  2 teaspoons garlic powder
  2 teaspoons paprika
  1 pinch of cayenne
  ½ teaspoon salt
  A dash of Tabasco

1. Place all the ingredients in a large bowl and mix them together well. (You'll have to use your hands, so make sure you wash off the grease from the piston rings of that '58 Ford engine you've been rebuilding.) Shape the mixture into patties about 4 inches across and 1 inch high.

2. Get the charcoal started. When the coals have ashed over, spread them evenly over the bottom of the grill. Place the turkey burgers in a hinged grill and cook them until they are lightly brown on the bottom, about 6 minutes. Turn and cook them 5 to 6 minutes more until they have lost their pinkness in the center. Serve on a soft roll, garnished just as you would a hamburger.

Note

Because they have less fat than hamburgers, turkey burgers do well cooked in a frying pan on the stove. Use 1 tablespoon of vegetable oil and let the pan get very hot before cooking the burgers 6 minutes on one side and then turning and cooking 5 to 6 minutes more.

Sicilian Potato Salad

Makes 8 servings

I have an aversion to potato salads with mayonnaise dressing. This salad uses olive oil and other ingredients you would find in a market in Palermo.

3 pounds new potatoes

1 red bell pepper, peeled, seeded, and coarsely diced

2 celery stalks, cut into ¼-inch slices

1 small red onion, cut in half lengthwise and sliced very thinly

8 sun-dried tomatoes packed in oil, drained and cut into thin slices

12 black olives, seeded and thinly sliced

4 anchovy fillets, finely chopped

2 whole scallions, chopped

¼ cup olive oil

10 fresh basil leaves, cut into large pieces; or 2 teaspoons dried

¼ cup chopped fresh parsley

1 teaspoon salt

Freshly ground black pepper

Note

You can replace the 2 tablespoons of olive oil with the oil from the sun-dried tomatoes for added flavor.

1. Scrub the potatoes and place them in a pot of cold water that covers them by about two inches. Bring the water to a boil over medium-high heat, and then reduce the heat so the water just simmers. Gentle boiling helps keep the potatoes from cracking and turning mealy. Boil the potatoes until they are just cooked through, about 12 minutes. Drain the potatoes in a colander and let them cool.

2. After the potatoes have cooled, cut them into quarters and transfer them to a large mixing bowl. Add the remaining ingredients and mix together. Refrigerate until ready to serve.

Grilled Zucchini

Makes 8 servings

8 medium zucchini
½ cup olive oil
¼ cup basil leaves, chopped; or 1 tablespoon dried

½ teaspoon salt
Freshly ground black pepper

1. Clean the zucchini by rinsing it in cold water and drying it with a towel. Trim the stems and cut the zucchini in half lengthwise. Place the zucchini in a shallow bowl and pour on the rest of the ingredients. Mix them around gently so that each piece is coated lightly with oil.

2. Place the zucchini on a hot grill, cut side down. Cook until it is lightly browned, about 4 minutes. Turn and cook 3 to 4 minutes more.

Note

For a more colorful presentation, you can substitute half the zucchini with yellow squash.

Basic Grilling Techniques

Grilling is not a passive activity. Laying the food on the barbecue and hoping that it will all cook while you meditate under a tree will not cut it. Grills are not uniformly hot. One area inevitably cooks the food faster than another. This requires you to shift the food so that each piece will be done at the same time. Another thing you have to deal with is flare-ups caused by dripping fat. The best way to deal with flaming coals is to quickly cover the grill for 10- to 20-second intervals. This smothers the fire and allows the fat to cook off.

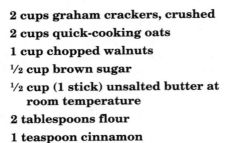

Apple-Blueberry Crisp

Makes 8 servings

The expression "easy as apple pie" should really be "easy as apple crisp." Adding the blueberries only makes it easier because you don't have to peel them.

2 cups graham crackers, crushed

2 cups quick-cooking oats

1 cup chopped walnuts

½ cup brown sugar

½ cup (1 stick) unsalted butter at room temperature

2 tablespoons flour

1 teaspoon cinnamon

4 large tart apples, such as Macintosh, Granny Smith, or Fuji

3 pints fresh or frozen blueberries

2 tablespoons unbleached, all-purpose flour

1 cup maple syrup

1. Preheat the oven to 350°F. In a medium mixing bowl, mix together the graham crackers, oats, walnuts, brown sugar, butter, flour, and cinnamon with your fingers until they are well combined. The mixture should resemble coarse meal when it is done.

2. Lightly grease a 9x12-inch baking dish. Peel the apples. Cut them into quarters, and then cut away the core section. Cut each quarter lengthwise into three slices.

3. Arrange the apples in an even layer over the bottom of the pan. Top the apples with half the graham-cracker mixture.

4. Place the blueberries in a mixing bowl, add the flour, and toss the blueberries so that they are lightly coated. Arrange the blueberries in an even layer in the pan and top with the remaining graham cracker mixture. Pour the syrup over the top and bake on the center rack for 35 minutes. Let cool before serving. This is a slightly messy dessert, so don't be disappointed if you can't cut it into perfect slices.

drinks

Make a fruit punch for the kids with equal parts grape, cranberry, orange, and pineapple juice and put it in a pitcher with a lot of ice.

Rum Punch

Makes 8 drinks

Make sure that you keep this one separate from the punch kids are drinking.

1 cup orange juice, preferably freshly squeezed
1 cup grapefruit juice, preferably freshly squeezed
$\frac{1}{2}$ cup pineapple juice
1 cup dark rum, preferably Meyer's
$\frac{1}{2}$ cup brandy
1 orange, thinly sliced
8 Maraschino cherries
8 paper umbrellas

1. Mix the orange juice, grapefruit juice, pineapple juice, rum, and brandy in a pitcher and add plenty of ice.

2. Pour into a tall glass and garnish with an orange slice, cherry, and little paper umbrella.

Dad Throws a Cocktail Party

Recipes make 16 servings

Despite opinions to the contrary, cocktail parties do serve a purpose—they allow a select group of people to meet who might not otherwise have the opportunity to get together socially—making small talk about gas mileage, attic insulation, soybean futures, and, I have just one word for you: plastics. These are folks you may know from work, church, synagogue, a book club, or the regular crew you share a table with at Tuesday night bingo. There also may be an acquaintance or client who you would like to know better but don't yet feel comfortable enough to ask out to dinner. Cocktail parties also are excellent opportunities to fix people up, for dates, perhaps, or business deals that could wind up helping you in the long run.

Sixteen is a nice number for this kind of party. Enough people for everyone to find someone to talk to but not too many that it becomes completely unmanageable. The menu consists of three cold appetizers and two hot. This should allow you time to do a fair amount of mingling, but always gives you an excuse to duck into the kitchen in order to escape a particularly tedious conversation. I highly recommend that you hire someone to help out for the evening, either in the kitchen or at the bar or both.

For better or worse, it definitely will get you some return invitations to other cocktail parties. And when it's done and you've scraped the last cocktail napkin off the furniture, you'll have a true feeling of accomplishment.

MeNu

Pita Triangles with Tapenade and Parmesan

Sautéed Shiitake Mushrooms

Smoked Salmon with Dill on English Cucumbers

Negimaki

Shrimp with Spicy Cocktail Sauce

Sea Breezes

Pita Triangles with Tapenade and Parmesan

Note

You also can serve crackers, such as Carr's or Stoned Wheat Thins, or flat bread along with the pita triangles.

Makes 16 servings as an appetizer

Tapenade is an earthy spread made with olives and anchovies. It's a unique flavor that your guests might not have had before. You will need a food processor to make this dish.

1 pound Kalamata olives, pitted

4 anchovy filets

1 clove garlic, mashed

2 tablespoons extra-virgin olive oil

8 pita rounds

4 ounces grated Parmesan cheese, preferably Parmigiano Reggiano

Cocktail piano and soft tenor sax make sense at this party. The following discs are suitable and musical enough so that you can listen to them when there's not a slew of guests chattering in your living room:

Tommy Flanagan: *Jazz Poet*
Zoot Sims: *If I'm Lucky*
Bill Evans: *Polka Dots and Moonbeams*
Frank Morgan: *You Must Believe in Spring*
Duke Ellington: *Small Group Sessions*

1. Place the pitted olives in the bowl of a food processor fitted with a metal blade. Add the anchovies, garlic, and olive oil and process until the mixture is somewhat smooth but still has small bits of olive intact. Do not process into a paste. Transfer the tapenade to a small serving bowl.

2. Cut the pita rounds into triangles and arrange them in a small basket lined with a decorative napkin. Put the Parmesan in another small serving bowl. To serve, place a butter knife in the tapenade and a small spoon in the Parmesan and arrange the bowls on a table next to the basket of pita.

Sautéed Shiitake Mushrooms

Makes 16 servings as an appetizer

I've served these everywhere from Fifth Avenue soirees to East Village gallery openings, and the blue-haired ladies and the blue-haired boys ate them up. The mushrooms have a subtle yet distinctive flavor that only needs gentle enhancing with the butter, wine, and bouillon.

1 pound shiitake mushrooms, stemmed

2 tablespoons butter

½ cup white wine

1 bouillon cube, cut in half

1. Cut any mushroom that is larger than a silver dollar in half.

2. Place a large frying pan on medium-high heat, add 1 tablespoon of the butter, and spread the butter so that it glazes the bottom of the pan. When the butter stops sizzling, add half the shiitake mushrooms and cook, stirring frequently, until they are soft, about 4 minutes.

3. Add ¼ cup of the wine and half the bouillon cube, breaking up the cube with a wooden spoon until it dissolves in the liquid. Stir the mushrooms in the pan so that they are coated with the sauce.

4. Remove the pan from the heat and insert toothpicks at a slight angle into the center of each mushroom at its thickest point. Arrange the mushrooms on a platter and serve as soon as they are cool enough to eat.

5. Wipe out the pan and repeat the steps when you are ready to serve these again.

Note

To facilitate serving the mushrooms during the party, cook them and then transfer to a small casserole or aluminum pan and cover it with foil. Just before the party starts, place it in an oven at 225°F to keep the mushrooms warm.

Hiring Help

Having someone in the kitchen making up the platters of food or roaming through picking up empty glasses or tending bar would be very helpful. Call a local caterer, preferably one you've used or that has been recommended, and ask them to suggest someone. If you know anyone who owns or works in a restaurant, they also might be able to help you out. One experienced assistant will make your party go a lot smoother.

Smoked Salmon with Dill on English Cucumbers

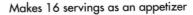

Makes 16 servings as an appetizer

These are simple, elegant, colorful, and not too fattening—all of which make them an appropriately swell appetizer to serve at your party.

2 English (also called *hothouse* or *seedless*) cucumbers

4 ounces sour cream or light sour cream

¾ pound smoked salmon, cut into ½-inch pieces

1 bunch fresh dill or parsley

Note

You can prepare these up to 1 hour before the party. Lay some lightly damp sheets of paper towel gingerly over the prepared slices and place the pan gently in the refrigerator. Garnish with the dill or parsley just before serving.

1. Rinse and dry the cucumbers and cut them on a slight angle into ¾-inch slices.

2. Use a melon baller or teaspoon to dig out a shallow crater in the center of each slice—about ½ inch across. Arrange the slices crater-side up on a cookie sheet.

3. Scoop out a teaspoon of sour cream and use a second teaspoon to edge a dollop about the size of a chocolate chip into each crater.

4. Arrange about a 1-inch piece of salmon next to the sour cream. Garnish with a small sprig of dill or parsley.

Negimaki

Negimaki is a Japanese dish made with thinly sliced beef rolled around scallions. This is the one appetizer that will take you away from your guests for a few minutes while you prepare it, but when you walk back in with the final product, the aroma, redolent of soy and ginger, will more than make up for your absence.

1½ pounds flank steak

12 scallions

½ cup soy sauce

½ cup Japanese Mirin cooking wine, or ½ cup white wine and 2 tablespoons brown sugar

1 tablespoon sesame oil

1 tablespoon fresh ginger, finely chopped

1 teaspoon garlic powder

4 tablespoons vegetable oil

1. Cut the steak on the bias into thin slices about 4 inches across. Putting the meat in the freezer for about ½ hour before you cut it makes this job easier.

2. Cut the green parts of the scallions into 1½-inch pieces. Mix together the soy sauce, wine, sesame oil, ginger, and garlic in a small mixing bowl and set aside.

3. Wrap one slice of meat around two pieces of scallion and secure it through the middle with a toothpick. Repeat with all the meat slices.

4. Heat 2 tablespoons of the vegetable oil in a large, heavy skillet until it is very hot (about 1½ minutes), spreading the oil so that it evenly glazes the bottom. Place 16 negimaki in the pan and cook them until the bottoms are brown, about 3 minutes. Turn them over and cook 3 minutes more.

5. Pour ⅓ of the soy sauce mixture into the pan. It will steam up, so be careful. Use a spatula to move and turn the negimaki so that they are coated with the sauce, about 30 seconds. Turn off the heat and remove the negimaki to a serving platter. Repeat steps 4 and 5 when it's time to serve another round of negimaki. Let them cool a minute before serving.

Shrimp with Spicy Cocktail Sauce

Makes 16 servings as an appetizer

If I've cleaned one shrimp, I've cleaned ten thousand—their guts, the little black band of guano politely called the "vein," scraped onto hundreds of paper towels like so many Jackson Pollocks. Unfortunately, some mysterious combination of divine and mortal forces converged to make shrimp expensive and difficult to peel. Otherwise, we'd eat them at almost every meal. Shrimp is an essential component of any cocktail party. This is my version of the classic cocktail sauce. But don't set out the shrimp right away because the first guests to arrive will gobble them all up.

2 pounds large shrimp, cleaned and deveined

2 tablespoons freshly squeezed lemon juice (1 lemon)

2 tablespoons freshly squeezed lime juice (1 lime)

1 tablespoon chili powder

2 teaspoons garlic powder

2 teaspoons salt

1 teaspoon freshly ground black pepper

¾ cup ketchup

¾ cup medium spicy salsa

1½ tablespoons red horseradish

1. Bring 6 quarts of water to a boil in a large pot. Add the shrimp and boil it until it is just cooked through, about 3 minutes. The outside should be pinkish and the inside opaque.

> ### Note
>
> If you are using frozen, cleaned shrimp, follow the instructions for thawing on the package and proceed with the recipe.

2. Drain the shrimp and rinse them in cold water until they cool down, about 2 minutes. Drain the shrimp well, pat them dry with a paper towel, and transfer them to a medium mixing bowl. Add the lemon juice, lime juice, chili powder, garlic powder, salt, and pepper and toss the shrimp gently so that they are all lightly coated. Let the shrimp marinate for 1 hour in the refrigerator.

> ### TIP
>
> Cut a lemon in half and then trim one of the ends so that it will sit flat. Place this on the shrimp platter with a few picks stuck in it so that the guests will get the idea of where to put their used timber.

3. Combine the ketchup, salsa, and horseradish in a small bowl and mix until combined.

4. Arrange the shrimp on a platter and place a toothpick in each one. Place a small, decorative bowl in the center of the platter for the sauce.

drinks

Besides the usual white and red wine so prevalent at cocktail parties, you might want to offer a more exotic drink. This one is especially appropriate in the spring or summer.

Sea Breeze

Makes 1 cocktail

Spring and summer parties are improved by serving these fruity cocktails. Using freshly squeezed grapefruit juice not only makes for better flavor but enhances the color.

$1\frac{3}{4}$ ounces vodka (about $2\frac{1}{2}$ tablespoons)
4 ounces fresh grapefruit juice ($\frac{1}{2}$ cup)
2 ounces cranberry juice ($\frac{1}{4}$ cup)

1. Mix the grapefruit juice and vodka together over ice.
2. Slowly pour the cranberry over the top, making a kind of sunset effect.

Presentation

Decorating the platters is an art in itself. But if you're not going to make a career out of it, it's best to keep it simple. Here are a few tips:

A flower blossom is the easiest way to perk up a tray. Lay an iris or an orchid along one side of the platter and arrange the appetizer in neat rows next to it.

Arrange chive stems in a checkerboard pattern on the tray and arrange the food in squares.

Do not cram the platters. On the other hand, you don't want them too sparse, or you'll be refilling them all the time.

Use platters with contrasting colors to the food, so that the food will look prettier.

How Much Wine and Liquor?

The caterer's rule of thumb is one drink per person per hour. This seems to balance out the guests who imbibe a lot with those who nurse one drink during the entire party.

For 16 people, the following amounts certainly will cover you for the party, and also will leave you with some left over to stock the liquor cabinet:

5 bottles white wine

3 bottles red wine

1 fifth vodka

1 fifth bourbon

1 fifth gin

1 fifth Scotch

1 small bottle vermouth

5 quarts sparkling water

2 quarts tonic

2 quarts grapefruit juice

2 quarts orange juice

1 quart cranberry juice

1 quart ginger ale

1 quart diet cola

2 limes, cut into small sections

1 lemon cut into twists

12 pounds of ice

About ¾ pound of ice per person should be sufficient for making drinks. If you need to keep the white wine on ice as well, you'll need about 10 pounds more.

Other Things You'll Need

20 wine glasses

16 cocktail glasses

16 highball glasses

4 dozen cocktail napkins

Round toothpicks

Serving platters (at least 12)

Wine Selections

For a party, you probably want to serve a decent white and red wine, but because you need to serve a lot of it, it should be economical as well. Here are some whites and reds in the $4 to $7 a bottle range. Refrain from getting magnums, however. Even though they might save you a few dollars, they are definitely *declassé*.

White Wines

B & G *Vin de Pays* Chardonnay (France)
Columbia Crest Chardonnay (Washington State)
Domaine de Pouy (France)
Mountainview Chardonnay (California)
Vendage Chardonnay (California)

Red Wines

Antinori *Santa Cristina Red* (Italy)
Glen Ellen *Proprietor's Reserve* Merlot (California)
Monterey Classic Merlot (California)
Mountainview Pinot Noir (California)

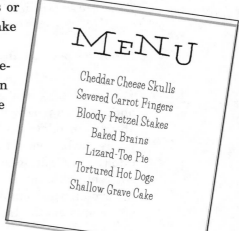

Halloween Party

Recipes serve 6 adults and 8 kids

Beware. Hosting a Halloween party for your kids can be the ultimate nightmare, or it can be lots of fun. Terrifying fun. The following is the translation of an ancient Egyptian text that details some haunting activities and gross-looking but tasty food. A few hours of work in the kitchen and a quick stop at the hobby and art supply stores ensure that anything frightful at the party happens on purpose. After the party, it's time for the kids to go trick or treating, torture the neighbors, and bring back bags of candy. That's when the real horror begins.

Halloween food has to look scary but taste great. Three creepy appetizers greet the guests when they arrive. Cheese skulls, severed carrot fingers, and vampire-killing pretzel stakes should keep them busy while they're making their witches hats and working on their magic spells. Your kids should get a kick out of helping to create these monstrous edibles, like putting the fingernails in the carrot fingers or adding the dried currants to the cheese skulls to make the empty eye sockets.

Even though the main course is also pretty revolting, if you accompany the meal with some plain old steamed broccoli or string beans, *that* will be what really makes the kids recoil in horror.

MeNu

Cheddar Cheese Skulls
Severed Carrot Fingers
Bloody Pretzel Stakes
Baked Brains
Lizard-Toe Pie
Tortured Hot Dogs
Shallow Grave Cake

Cheddar Cheese Skulls

Makes 12 servings as an appetizer

One 10-ounce Cheddar cheese brick

4 ounces dried currants

1. Cut the Cheddar brick into about twenty-four ¼-inch square slices. Trim each slice into a peanut-shaped skull (See drawing).

2. Place dried currants on each slice to make the eyes, nose, and mouth holes. (The kids can help with this.)

3. Arrange the skulls on a platter and garnish with a plastic lizard or small rodent.

Severed Carrot Fingers

Makes 12 servings as an appetizer

These are easy to assemble using the peeled baby carrots that are now widely available. Sliced almonds serve as fingernails.

12 ounces peeled baby carrots

4 ounces sliced almonds

1. Holding the carrot upright and being attentive not to confuse it with your pinkie, use a paring knife to carefully cut down into the top, making a slit about ¾ inch long, as if you were cutting behind your own fingernail. Then, where the bottom of the fingernail would be, about ½ inch from the top, cut into the first slit. Remove the sliver of carrot and you should have a ¼-inch slit remaining into which you slip one of the almond slices to resemble a fingernail. This sounds more complicated than it really is. Once you try it, you should get the hang of it very quickly.

2. Arrange the fingers on serving platters and garnish with a gory Halloween figure or some plastic bugs.

Bloody Pretzel Stakes

Makes 2 dozen

If you have any neighbors with dirt from Transylvania in a coffin in their basement, see if you can borrow some to use as an authentic garnish.

24 pretzel logs, plus a few extra in case of breakage

1 ounce red food coloring

1. Carefully sharpen one end of the pretzel log on a cheese grater using the smallest side. Don't try to make super-sharp points or the pretzels will break.

2. Dip the sharpened tip into a small bowl of red food coloring.

3. Arrange on a platter or any small coffin you might have lying around.

Tortured Hot Dogs

Makes 8 servings

12 hot dogs

½ cup ketchup

3 to 4 ounces Cheddar cheese, cut into dime-size pieces

1. Preheat the oven to 350°F. Arrange the hot dogs on a baking pan. Cut several slits into the hot dogs and insert the pieces of cheese. Bake them on the center rack for 15 to 20 minutes until they are heated through.

2. Transfer to a platter, letting the cheese ooze and fester. Garnish with Type A positive ketchup.

Baked Brains

This dish is basically ground turkey meat loaf baked in a pasta shell. It's actually a variation of an elegant French terrine which you might pay a lot of money for in a Paris restaurant. There, instead of ground turkey it would be filled with veal and fois gras. It's worth seeking out the cavatelli because they really do resemble gray matter after they're baked. This recipe might sound strange, but it tastes great.

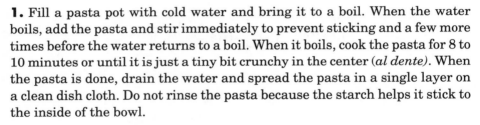

8 ounces cavatelli pasta or elbow macaroni

4 slices of white or oatmeal bread

¼ cup of milk

1½ pounds ground turkey

¼ cup ketchup

1 egg

1 tablespoon garlic powder

½ teaspoon salt

1. Fill a pasta pot with cold water and bring it to a boil. When the water boils, add the pasta and stir immediately to prevent sticking and a few more times before the water returns to a boil. When it boils, cook the pasta for 8 to 10 minutes or until it is just a tiny bit crunchy in the center (*al dente*). When the pasta is done, drain the water and spread the pasta in a single layer on a clean dish cloth. Do not rinse the pasta because the starch helps it stick to the inside of the bowl.

2. Preheat the oven to 350°F. Butter the inside of a 2½-quart stainless or glass oven-proof mixing bowl (about 9½ inches across) and refrigerate it.

3. In a large mixing bowl, combine the bread and milk and let it soak for a minute. Add the ground turkey, ketchup, egg, garlic powder, and salt to the bowl and mix together with your fingers until it is well combined. Set aside.

4. Remove the buttered bowl from the refrigerator and line it with a single layer of pasta, packed as tightly as possible. Spoon the turkey mixture into the pasta cavity and gently pat down the meat. Cover the bowl with aluminum foil and place it in a 2-inch-deep baking pan. Fill the pan with hot water and put it on the center rack of the oven. (Cooking the brains in the water bath keeps the pasta from drying out.) Bake for 1 hour or until the meat loses its pinkness. Let the brains cool for 5 minutes before inverting the bowl onto a platter. Remove the bowl and serve immediately.

Lizard-Toe Pie

Makes 6 servings

Lizard toe is the kind of thing you can find in one of the apothecaries in New York's Chinatown. But if you can't get there and your local market doesn't stock pureed lizard toe, I recommend using frozen creamed spinach.

One 6-ounce package of chopped spinach

Two 12-ounce packages frozen creamed spinach

1 cup grated Cheddar cheese

DRINKS

Cranberry juice is a must for this meal. You can then give it an appropriately creepy name: Vampire Cocktail, Transfusion Punch, Artery Juice, etc.

1. Preheat the oven to 350°F. Lightly butter a deep pie dish or 8x8-inch baking dish.

2. Boil the chopped spinach in a medium saucepan, drain it in a colander, and cool it under cold water. Drain again, squeeze out the excess water, and set aside. While the chopped spinach is cooking, cook the creamed spinach in a separate saucepan. When it is done, transfer it to a medium mixing bowl. Add the chopped spinach to the creamed spinach along with the cheddar cheese and stir until well combined.

3. Use a rubber spatula to transfer the mixture to the prepared pan. Bake on the center rack of the oven for 40 minutes. Let it cool for 10 minutes before serving, so that none of the young ghouls burn their mouths.

Shallow Grave Cake

Makes 12 to 16 servings

The idea here is to create something resembling a grave out of two layers of chocolate cake. If a vampire had a sweet tooth, Shallow Grave cake is what he'd have for dessert.

4 cups cake flour

1¼ cups cocoa

4 teaspoons baking powder

1 teaspoon baking soda

1¼ cups butter (2½ sticks) at room temperature

3 cups granulated sugar

4 large eggs

1 cup warm water

1⅓ cups milk

1 tablespoon vanilla extract

Two 12-ounce cans chocolate frosting

One 8-ounce tube marzipan (for gravestone)

1 teaspoon red food coloring (for garnish)

¾ pound green gummy worms or green candy ribbons (for garnish)

1. Preheat the oven to 350°F. Generously grease two 9x12-inch baking pans or aluminum lasagna pans, line the bottom with wax paper, and lightly grease the wax paper. In a large mixing bowl, stir together the flour, cocoa, baking powder, and baking soda with a whisk until they are well combined.

Elvira's collection of oddball novelty songs would be just about right to accompany this party. There you can find hits like "Monster Mash" and "They're Coming To Take Me Away."

2. In a medium mixing bowl, cream together the butter and sugar with an electric mixer on medium speed until the mixture is smooth and pale yellow, about 3 minutes. Add the eggs, water, milk, and vanilla and beat until well combined, about 1 minute.

3. Add the dry ingredients and continue mixing until all the ingredients are incorporated. Then beat for 3 more minutes on high speed, periodically scraping down the bowl.

4. Divide the batter equally between the two baking pans. Bake the cakes on the center rack of the oven for 22 to 27 minutes or until a toothpick inserted in the center comes out clean. Let the cake cool for 45 minutes before assembling the grave.

5. To make the grave, remove the cakes from the pans and place one cake on a platter. Cover it with a thin layer of chocolate frosting and then place the second layer on top. Use a serrated knife to trim the cake into a mound resembling a grave. Then cover the whole cakes with a thin layer of chocolate frosting.

6. You can make a gravestone with the marzipan. An 8-ounce tube of marzipan makes a 5x6-inch rectangle for the gravestone. Use the point of a skewer to carve the letters RIP into the marzipan. If you've never worked with marzipan, it's just like Playdough. You also can decorate the stone with some drops of red food coloring dripping down to resemble blood. Gummy worms and green candy ribbons can make up grass around the freshly dug earth.

Fun and Games

Most Creative Spell Contest

Here the kids devise a fabulously revolting spell to cast on an unsuspecting victim. We photocopied a sheet like this for each kid. Nonreaders were assisted.

I, Witch _____, call upon the Demon of the Dark named _____ to put a spell on _____ because they _____ me. To cast this wicked spell, which will make their _____ fall off and their _____ turn _____, I will put in my witches' cauldron the following items. (Here you list what you'll use in your spell.)

And now I will say the magic words to make the spell take effect. (Here you make up your magic words.)

Homemade Witches Hats

This is the method sanctioned by the Cardboard Witches Hat Association of America. No Halloween party is complete without them. It takes a few minutes for the paint to dry, so you might want to assemble these in stages:

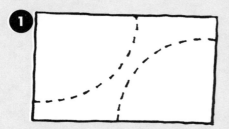

2. Cut two semicircles with an 18-inch radius from opposite corners of a 24x36-inch piece of black oaktag paper. (See drawing 1.)

1. Cut a circle of corrugated cardboard 2 feet in diameter. We used the sides of boxes for this. Paint both sides of the circle witches black using any kind of water-based paint.

3. Shape the oaktag into a cone and tape the seam with a strip of wide black cloth tape. (See drawing 2.)

4. When the paint is dry, place the cone on the center of the cardboard circle and trace around the bottom. Using a mat knife and starting at the center of the circle, cut about 16 slits from the center to the edge of the circle you traced around the bottom of the cone. The slits should be about 1 inch apart, like thin pieces of pie. (See drawing 3.)

5. Push the cone up through the center until the bottom is even with the cardboard. A few pieces of tape will secure it in place and *viola!* Now all you need is to practice your sinister witch's voice—"I'll get you, my pretty. And your little dog, too!" (See drawings 4 and 5.)

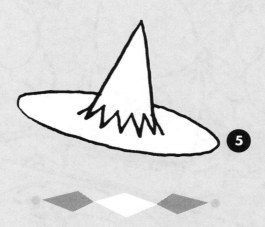

Guess What You're Touching
(the PG version)

Hollow out a bunch of medium-size pumpkins and place some incredibly yucky but nontoxic stuff inside, like overcooked macaroni, butterscotch pudding, and a smoked pig's foot. Blindfolded guests put their hands in each pumpkin, trying to guess what they are touching. If you don't want to use pumpkins, you can cut a hole in the side of a shoebox or other small cardboard box.

Lobster Boil

Recipes make 6 servings

Finding fault with boiled lobster is like finding fault with Ernie Banks or Veronica Lake or Patricia Highsmith or Sonny Rollins. What's the point? Sure, there is such a thing as lousy lobster, usually at summer resort restaurants where the college kid spending the summer "cooking" throws the barely 1 pounder into the pot, hits on the waitress for the next half-hour, and forgets to take it out.

But at home, you can spring for BIG ones, $1\frac{1}{2}$ to $2\frac{1}{2}$ pounders, with tails so formidable they belong in the Museum of Natural History. And because you have so much invested, you will cook them perfectly. You then will serve them to guests who you've chosen specifically because you want something in return. Maybe one belongs to a golf club whose course you've been itching to play, one has a 20-foot sailboat docked nearby, or one has a pool in the backyard. A $1\frac{1}{2}$ pounder should get you a few laps at least, because this is the kind of meal that tends to get people forever in your debt. Start listing the return favors you have in mind while the water is boiling. You can begin with having them watch your kids for the weekend.

Of course there's always the chance that one of your guests could be squeamish about eating lobsters, thinking about their being alive only minutes before dinner. So make sure you alert all those you've invited to exactly what's on the menu.

MENU

Manhattan Clam Chowder
Irish Soda Bread
Steamed Lobsters
Potato and Shiitake Mushroom Tart
Blueberry Surprise

Manhattan Clam Chowder

Makes 6 servings

I've left the potatoes out of this chowder because we're having them later in the meal—I've substituted corn instead. Using the prosciutto adds a subtler flavor to the soup than the traditional bacon.

1 tablespoon vegetable oil

⅛ pound prosciutto slices, cut into ½-inch pieces

1 medium onion, diced

1 stalk celery, diced

1 carrot, diced

2 cloves garlic, minced

Two 12-ounce cans minced clams, including liquid

One 6-ounce bottle clam juice

One 28-ounce can whole peeled tomatoes, including liquid

2 chicken bouillon cubes

1 teaspoon paprika

½ teaspoon dried thyme

One 8-ounce package frozen corn

Wine Selections
A dry, crisp white wine is a pleasant accompaniment to the lobster. An Alsacian Reisling or French Muscadet served very cold would be just right. Some Reislings to consider are Trimbach, Hugel, or the more expensive Boxler.

1. Heat the oil in a heavy-bottomed soup pot over medium-high heat until it is hot, about 1 minute, spreading the oil so that it evenly glazes the bottom. Add the prosciutto and cook, stirring frequently, until it is heated through, about 1 minute. Add the onion, celery, and carrot and cook, stirring frequently, until they are soft, about 5 minutes. Add the garlic and cook 1 minute more.

2. Add the clams and their liquid, the clam juice, whole tomatoes and their liquid, and the bouillon cubes to the pot and bring the liquid to a boil, breaking up the whole tomatoes with the side of a mixing spoon.

3. When the liquid boils, reduce the heat to medium-low and simmer the soup, covered, for 15 minutes. Stir in the paprika, thyme, and corn and continue cooking until the corn is heated through, about 3 more minutes.

Irish Soda Bread

Makes 2 loaves

Authentic Irish soda bread from Boston is perfect to dip in the Manhattan-style clam chowder. This juxtaposition reflects my own personal heritage, having been born outside Boston, where we would say, "Pahs the chow-dah," and living now in New York, where we say, "Pass the f—ing chowder."

4 cups unbleached, all-purpose flour

⅔ cup sugar

1 tablespoon baking powder

1¾ cup buttermilk

1 cup dried currants

2 tablespoons butter, melted

2 extra-large eggs, lightly beaten

1. Preheat the oven to 350°F. Lightly grease a large baking pan.

2. In a large mixing bowl, stir together the flour, sugar, and baking powder with a whisk until they are well combined.

3. In a medium bowl, stir together the buttermilk, currants, melted butter, and eggs until they are well combined.

4. Pour the buttermilk mixture into the flour mixture and stir slowly but deliberately until the flour mixture is completely moistened. Do not over mix.

5. Divide the dough in half and shape into 2 round loaves and put them on the baking sheet, about 6 inches apart. Bake the bread on the center rack of the oven until the top is golden brown and a toothpick inserted in the center comes out clean, about 50 to 55 minutes. Gently transfer the breads to a wire rack to cool for 20 minutes before slicing and serving.

Steamed Lobsters

Makes 6 servings

This is called a lobster boil, but you are actually going to steam the lobsters, which helps keep the meat tender and moist. Unless you have a large stock pot, you probably will need two pasta pots to be able to cook the lobsters all at once. Make sure they both have a tight-fitting lid.

2 cups white wine

1 cup clam juice

2 bay leaves

1 medium onion, peeled and cut in half

1 celery stalk, rinsed and cut in half

1 carrot, rinsed and cut in half

Juice of 1 lemon, plus the rind

Six 1½ to 2½-pound lobsters (see A Few Words on Lobsters)

1. Place all the ingredients except the lobsters in a stockpot, 20 quarts minimum, and bring to a boil over high heat. Immediately reduce the heat to low, cover the pot, and simmer for 10 minutes. This extracts some of the flavor from the vegetables.

2. Increase the heat to high, add the lobsters, and immediately cover the pot. As soon as the liquid comes to a boil, reduce the heat to medium low and steam the lobsters for 18 minutes for 1½-pound lobsters and 2 more minutes for each additional ¼ pound. The best way to handle a lobster is to hold onto the body right behind the claws.

3. Remove the lobsters with tongs and place on the dinner plates. Serve with small bowls of melted butter. Cut the rubber bands holding their claws shut.

Note

You might want to put on some loud music when you put the live lobsters in the pot so that you won't hear any sounds coming from inside.

You might have to invest in some nutcrackers and lobster picks. Both are essential for getting at the meat and because you're not using these lobsters in a still life, it's probably a good idea to have them on hand. Once you own them, it will be that much easier to make lobster again.

A Few Words on Lobsters

Lobsters shed their shells in the summer and, in so doing, take on a lot of water. Summer lobsters tend to be less meaty and soggy. The old adage of eating lobsters only in months with "R"s in them still holds true. During these months, the shells have hardened and the lobster has shed its excess water. Although there's a strong urge to host your Lobster Boil in the summer, it's best to wait until fall.

Make sure that your lobsters are packed in a paper bag for storage. If they are wrapped in plastic, they will suffocate. A reputable fish store will throw in some seaweed as well. Buy your lobsters the day you are cooking them and get them into the refrigerator as soon as you get home. They should keep there for up to 8 hours.

Potato and Shiitake Mushroom Tart

Makes 6 servings

You can never make enough of this sublime combination of potato and mushrooms.

5 large Idaho potatoes, peeled

2 tablespoons butter

3 shallots, finely chopped

6 ounces shiitake mushrooms, stemmed and thinly sliced

¼ cup (½ stick) butter, melted

Salt and freshly ground black pepper

1. Preheat the oven to 450°F. Using the single slicing blade on the side of a grater, grate the potatoes into thin slices. Try to get them as round and thin as you can, but don't worry if they're not perfect. After they are sliced, transfer them immediately to a bowl of cold water and set aside.

2. Place a medium frying pan over medium-high heat. Add the 2 tablespoons of butter to the pan and, as it starts sizzling, spread it so that it evenly glazes the bottom. Add the shallots and shiitake mushrooms and cook, stirring frequently until the mushrooms are soft, about 5 minutes. Turn off the heat and set aside.

3. Generously butter the inside of a pie pan with about a tablespoon of the melted butter. Drain the potatoes in a colander, lay them on a dish towel or paper towel and pat them dry. Transfer them to a mixing bowl and add the remaining melted butter, salt, and pepper. Toss the potatoes gently so that they are all coated with the butter.

4. Arrange a single layer of the potatoes in the pie pan. Spoon a third of the mushroom mixture over the potatoes. Arrange another layer of potatoes over the mushrooms, and top that with more mushrooms. Repeat the layering process until the potatoes are used up. Place a second pie plate or dinner plate that fits in snugly over the top layer of potatoes and push down very hard to press the layers together as tightly as possible. Remove the pie plate and replace any potato slices stuck to the bottom. Bake on the center rack for 45 minutes or until it is golden brown. Let the tart rest a few minutes before cutting it into 6 wedges and serving.

Blueberry Surprise

Makes 8 servings

I've always wanted to write the "Surprise Cookbook" where every recipe is a surprise. Liver and Onions Surprise, Lima Bean Surprise, Tripe Surprise and a Half. There's nothing actually surprising about this other than how easy it is to make.

1 pint blueberries

1 cup plus 2 tablespoons flour

½ cup plus 2 tablespoons sugar

1 tablespoon lemon juice

6 tablespoons butter, at room temperature; plus more to grease pan

1 egg

1 teaspoon vanilla

⅓ cup milk

2 teaspoons baking powder

Whipped cream for serving

1. Preheat the oven to 350°F. Generously butter 8 standard-size muffin tins.

2. Rinse the blueberries, drain them well, and transfer to a mixing bowl. Sprinkle on the 2 tablespoons of flour, 2 tablespoons of sugar, and the lemon juice and toss together.

3. Cream together the butter and the remaining sugar by stirring the two with a wooden spoon until the mixture is smooth and pale yellow, about 2 minutes. Stir in the egg and vanilla until it is completely incorporated. Then stir in the milk until it is completely incorporated.

4. In a separate mixing bowl, stir together the remaining flour, sugar, and baking powder with a whisk until they are well combined. Add the dry ingredients to the wet ingredients and stir until just combined. Do not over mix.

5. Fill the muffins tins ⅔ full with the blueberries. Spoon the batter over the berries to the top of the tin. Bake on the center rack of the oven until the tops are lightly brown, about 25 minutes. Let the surprises cool for a few minutes before transferring them to individual dessert plates. Serve with a dollop of whipped cream or some vanilla ice cream.

Note

You might not be able to remove the surprises cleanly from the tins, but you can reassemble them on the dessert plate and gussy them up with the whipped cream. You can make these a few hours before the guests arrive. Leave them in the tins and reheat them by placing the whole tin in a warm oven for a few minutes.

Lush Life

Recipes make 4 servings

You're not simply making a meal here—you're fashioning a memory, something legendary, a dinner that will become part of the lore. "Remember those morels?" It will become a milestone in your life. "Did that happen before The Meal, or after?" You will prepare food so spectacular that no one will believe you cooked it, especially if they know you well.

You'll need most of the day to prepare this dinner—the morning you'll shop, searching out the freshest possible ingredients. You might have to travel to more than one store, to find the morels, *haricots verts,* and better chocolate for the soufflé. You also might want to seek out a purveyor of organic or free-range chickens, which have sufficiently more flavor to merit the effort spent procuring them for this meal.

You'll spend the afternoon in the kitchen, cooking your buns off. Get the morels soaking, then cook the salmon cakes and assemble *aioli,* so that the cakes only need to be reheated before serving. Once the morels are ready, you can jump right into the cream sauce for the chicken. Get the ingredients assembled for the soufflé so that you can whip it together right before you serve the salmon. Prepare your wife or significant other for this, because she may have to hold down the fort conversation-wise while you're busy in the kitchen. Maybe you'll buy some special music to cook by. A new CD or cassette. Don't listen to the radio. The news might have a story on the latest health risks from too much fat and cholesterol. You won't want to hear them as you put this meal together. This dinner is opulent, expensive, and worth it.

MeNU

Salmon Cakes with Red Pepper Aioli
Wild Rice
Chicken with Morels and Cream Sauce
Haricot Verts
Chocolate Soufflé

Salmon Cakes with Red Pepper Aioli

Makes 4 servings

Don't mistake these for tuna patties. The salmon provides a subtle and distinct flavor and the aioli sauce finishes it off with some real panache.

For the *aioli*

1 roasted pepper, cored and
    seeded (see page 21), or one
    6-ounce jar roasted red peppers,
    drained

¼ cup unseasoned bread crumbs

2 egg yolks

1 clove garlic

1 cup olive oil

¾ cup vegetable oil

2 tablespoons canned chicken
    broth

For the salmon cakes

1 pound salmon fillet, cut into
    2-inch pieces

2 slices white or oatmeal bread,
    crusts removed and cut into
    2-inch pieces

1 large egg

½ medium red onion, coarsely
    chopped

3 cloves garlic, coarsely chopped

½ cup fresh parsley leaves

2 whole scallions cut into 1-inch
    pieces

A dash Tabasco

Chopped parsley (for garnish)
Lemon wedge (for garnish)
    4 tablespoons corn oil

Note

If you don't have a food processor,
you will have to spend a few minutes
with your chef's knife chopping the
salmon as finely as you can.

You can prepare the salmon cakes
up to 2 hours before the guests
arrive. Reheat them in a hot oven for
2 to 3 minutes before serving.

1. To make the *aioli,* place the roasted pepper, bread crumbs, egg yolks, and garlic in the bowl of a food processor fitted with metal blade or a blender and process until the mixture becomes a smooth paste, about 30 seconds. Slowly dribble in the oil in a thin, steady stream until all the oil is incorporated. This may take 3 to 4 minutes. Add the chicken broth 1 tablespoon at a time until the mixture is the consistency of mayonnaise. Refrigerate until ready to use.

2. To make the salmon cakes, place all the ingredients for the salmon cakes except the corn oil in the bowl of a food processor (see note) fitted with steel blade and pulse until the mixture is just mixed together and still slightly coarse, about 12 pulses. Transfer the salmon mixture to a bowl. Shape the mixture into 12 cakes about 2 inches across and place them on a baking sheet or large platter lined with wax paper.

3. Preheat the oven to 225°F. Heat 2 tablespoons of the corn oil in a large, heavy skillet until it is very hot, about 1½ minutes, spreading the oil so that it evenly glazes the bottom. Add 6 of the salmon cakes and cook until they are lightly brown, about 5 minutes. Turn and brown 5 minutes more. Transfer the cooked cakes to a baking pan or oven-proof platter, cover with aluminum foil, and place in the oven to keep warm. Repeat this process with the remaining 6 cakes.

4. To serve, place 3 salmon cakes on an appetizer plate, and spoon 2 to 3 tablespoons of the *aioli* on the plate between them. Garnish with a sprig of fresh parsley and a lemon wedge.

How to Set the Table

The following diagram shows the proper placement of the silverware, plate, and glasses for the meal. Set the table with the dinner plate as an underliner, place the appetizer plate on top when serving the salmon cakes, and then remove both plates before serving the chicken.

Wild Rice

Makes 4 servings

Not a true rice, wild rice is a nutty, flavorful grain that stands up to the morel sauce.

3 cups water   **6 ounces wild rice**
1 tablespoon butter

1. Place the water, butter, and rice in a medium saucepan with a tight-fitting lid. Bring the water to a boil over high heat.

2. As soon as the water boils, reduce the heat to low, cover the pan, and simmer until the rice is cooked through, about 50 minutes.

3. Fluff with a fork before serving.

Chicken with Morels and Cream Sauce

Makes 4 servings

Morels are the closest thing you can get to truffles. Some chefs even prefer the flavor of these dried mushrooms over a truffle. They certainly impart an earthy, intense flavor to the sauce. It might take a little doing to find the morels, although most specialty food shops should carry them. They're expensive, but that only adds to the drama of this meal. Note that the morels do require 2 hours of soaking before you can use them, so take that into account during your preparations.

1 ounce dried morels

1 cup warm water

2 tablespoons butter

3 shallots, finely chopped

1 clove garlic, finely chopped

¼ cup white wine

½ cup canned chicken broth, or
  ½ cup water and 1 bouillon cube

½ cup heavy cream

Salt and freshly ground black
  pepper

2 tablespoons olive oil

1 cup flour

4 boneless and skinless chicken
  breasts, 5 to 6 ounces each

Chopped fresh parsley for garnish

Note

The sauce can be prepared (through step 2) up to 24 hours before the dinner. Store in a well-sealed plastic container in the refrigerator. Reheat over low heat, thinning with a few tablespoons of cream if necessary.

1. Make the sauce. Soak the morels in the warm water for 2 hours before preparing the sauce. Remove the morels from the soaking liquid and let them dry for a minute on a paper towel. Save the soaking liquid by straining it through a fine-mesh strainer and set aside.

2. Place a large frying pan over medium-high heat. Add the butter to the pan and, as it starts sizzling, spread it so that it evenly glazes the bottom. Add the shallots and morels and cook, stirring continuously, until the shallots are soft, about 3 minutes. Add the garlic and cook 1 minute more. Add the wine and cook until it is reduced by half, about 1 minute. Add the chicken broth and ½ cup of the morel soaking liquid and cook until reduced by half, about 2 minutes. Add the cream and cook, stirring frequently, until the sauce is thick enough to coat the back of a spoon, about 3 minutes.

3. Measure the flour into a pie plate or shallow bowl. Lay each side of the chicken breast in the flour so that it is lightly coated, shaking gently to remove any excess. Transfer to a dinner plate.

4. For the chicken, heat the olive oil in a large, heavy skillet over medium-high heat until it is very hot, about 1½ minutes, spreading the oil so that it evenly glazes the bottom. Add the chicken breasts and cook until they are lightly brown, about 5 minutes. Turn and cook 4 minutes more. Season with salt and pepper.

5. To serve, place a chicken breast on a dinner plate along with some wild rice (page 213) and the *haricot verts* (recipe follows). Spoon a few tablespoons of sauce over the chicken, making sure to distribute the morels evenly. Garnish with a pinch of chopped fresh parsley.

Haricot Verts

Makes 4 servings

These are French-style string beans, thinner than the ones you're used to. Trim only the stem, but leave the squiggly tip intact.

8 ounces *haricot verts*
1 tablespoon butter
Salt and freshly ground black pepper

1. Clean the beans under cold water and pat them dry.

2. Place a medium skillet over a medium-high heat. Add the butter to the pan and, as it starts sizzling, spread it so that it evenly glazes the bottom. Add the beans and cook, stirring frequently, until they turn bright green and are just cooked through, about 2 minutes.

3. Season with salt and pepper.

drinks

Wine Selections

This meal calls for a fancy wine, preferably one from your guest's well-stocked cellar. But if your friends only have a washer, dryer, and a few leftover pieces of broadloom from when they carpeted the den a decade ago, you might have to get the wine yourself. If they do offer, guide them toward an appropriate bottle. The finest French whites are the Muersault, Puligny Montrachet, Chassagne Montrachet, and the Grand Cru Chablis. These bottles range from $15 to $40, depending on the vintage.

After-Dinner Sauternes

Delicately sweet, sipping a sauternes at the end of a meal is a sublime experience. Letting the refined, complex flavor of this linger on your taste buds is the perfect way to end the meal and will leave a sweet taste in your mouth as you retire to your chambers for the evening. Chateau d' Yguem has the reputation for producing the finest sauternes, though they are very expensive. You can find a worthy ½ bottle that will run about $20 to $30. Look for these makers or another that your wine merchant recommends:

Lafaurie Peyraguey
Roymond Lafon
Sigalas Rabaud
Suduirait

Chocolate Soufflé

Note

If you don't have an electric beater, you can use a whisk to beat the egg whites, which will take about 8 minutes. It's a good workout for the wrists and will help you turn on an inside fastball. Just make sure you wash the whisk well before using it. Any little bit of fat from the egg yolks will prevent the whites from whipping up.

Makes 8 servings

You probably think of soufflés as the joke dessert—the one Moe's wife was trying to make and Curly ruined by opening the oven too soon, deflating it like a punctured tire, which it probably was. But I feel it's time you made your first soufflé, and although it might not join the exclusive pantheon of major events in your life, such as getting your learner's permit or copping your first feel, when you see the looks of wonder from your guests upon presenting a warm chocolate soufflé for dessert, it will become an event of not insignificant proportion. You'll need to have a 2-quart soufflé dish for this recipe to come out right. Once you taste it, you'll be glad you have it around. The soufflé makes 8 servings, so if you want to invite a few extra guests for dessert, feel free. You can always wake up the kids. It will make a nice story to tell their class at school.

6 tablespoons butter

6 tablespoons unbleached, all-purpose flour

1½ cups whole milk

½ cup sugar

6 ounces best-quality bittersweet chocolate, such as Lindt, Valroohna, or Giradelli, broken into small pieces

9 eggs, separated (you will use 6 of the yolks and all of the whites)

1 tablespoon vanilla

Chocolate sauce (recipe follows)

1. Preheat the oven to 350°F. Generously butter a 2-quart soufflé dish. Fold a 30-inch piece of aluminum foil in half lengthwise and butter one side of it. Fit the foil around the soufflé dish so that it forms a 3-inch collar above the rim with the buttered side facing in. Secure it with a couple of folds or some cotton string.

2. Melt the butter in a 4-quart saucepan over medium heat. When it is just melted, sprinkle the flour into the pan and blend together with a whisk. Cook, stirring continuously, for 1 minute. Add the milk in a slow, steady stream and stir continuously over the heat until it is thickened and smooth, about 5 minutes.

3. Add the chocolate and the sugar to the pan and continue stirring until the chocolate is melted. Remove the pan from the heat and continuing to stir with the whisk until it cools slightly, about 2 minutes. Add the 6 egg yolks and vanilla to the chocolate mixture and whisk until they are incorporated.

4. In a separate bowl, beat the 9 egg whites with an electric beater until they are stiff but not dry. Use a large rubber spatula to fold the egg whites into the chocolate mixture. When they are just combined, use the spatula to transfer the mixture to the soufflé dish. Place the dish in a large baking pan filled with hot water and place it on the center rack of the oven. Bake for 45 minutes, or until the top is firm. Bring the soufflé to the table in its dish and serve it from there. Top with chocolate sauce.

MUSIC

This meal requires some majestic yet not overpowering music. Try Arturo Benedetti Michelangeli playing Debussy, Horowitz playing Chopin, Joe Pass playing solo guitar, or Sarah Vaughn singing ballads. This music has the subtle complexity that will stand up to a fine bottle of Muersault.

Chocolate Sauce

Makes 1 cup

So you can be with you guests as much as possible, make this sauce ahead of time. It can be reheated in a double boiler or briefly in the microwave just before serving.

6 ounces semisweet or bittersweet chocolate

3 tablespoons butter

¼ cup heavy cream

1. Melt the chocolate and butter in the top of a double boiler or a stainless-steel mixing bowl set over a saucepan of simmering water. Stir occasionally until the chocolate melts.

2. Add the heavy cream and stir until it is completely incorporated and the mixture is smooth. Turn off the heat but keep the sauce warm over the double boiler until you're ready to serve.

Eight Forks—One Pan

Recipes make 8 servings

The idea here is to make one dish so sumptuous, so overflowing with delectable ingredients that no one notices it's the only thing you're serving for the main course. The advantage to you is that instead of being confined to the kitchen for much of the party, you'll be shmoozing with your guests, listening to the saga of their putting the addition on the house, the latest refinement in a golf swing, or talk of a stock you, alas, really missed the boat on.

Likewise, you won't have to spend the whole day cooking. Use the morning to get the paella started and the late afternoon to get it ready to put in the oven. You easily can squeeze a game of tennis in the middle of the day, or take the kids for a bike ride, or buy your wife a new teddy. The first course is a simple yet delectable platter of carefully selected cheeses, olives, and breads, requiring no cooking at all. Once you shower and don your zoot suit with the reet pleats, you can greet your friends, linger in the living room, fix them a drink, let them show you the new grip they're using on their backhand, and empty the olive pits from the ashtrays. In short, enjoy yourself, confident that the paella—opulent with shrimp, chicken, and sausage—which you have cooking in the oven will be ready when you need it.

MENU

Appetizer Platter
Cherry Tomatoes with Herbed Vinaigrette
Paella Grande
Mushrooms and Garlic
Ice Cream with Tropical Fruit
Sangria

Appetizer Platter

Makes 8 servings

An easy way to create a respectable first course is to arrange some select tidbits culled from the shelves of your local gourmet shop. The following selection is in keeping with the Mediterranean origins of the paella. You'll need your nicest platter that's at least 12 inches across. If you've got one divided into sections that's not too tacky, perhaps a wedding gift you haven't looked at since you unpacked after your honeymoon at Niagara Falls, now's the time to use it.

½ **pound black olives, such as Calamata or Italian oil cured**

½ **pound green olives**

½ **pound wedge hard cheese, such as aged Gouda, extra-sharp Cheddar, or Fontina**

½ **pound soft cheese, such as herbed goat, Saga, or Tallegio**

12 **ounces bread sticks or flat bread**

1 **French bread, cut into 3/4-inch rounds**

1. Arrange the different items in wedges on the platter.

2. Place a stack of salad plates and forks to allow the guests to take what they want.

Cherry Tomatoes with Herbed Vinaigrette

Makes 8 servings as an appetizer

Serve these in a separate bowl next to the appetizer platter.

1 pound ripe cherry tomatoes

2 whole scallions, cut into 1-inch pieces

Leaves from 10 stems Italian parsley

2 tablespoons white wine vinegar

½ clove garlic

½ teaspoon salt

¼ teaspoon pepper

6 tablespoons olive oil

1. Clean the cherry tomatoes by rinsing them under cold water and patting them dry with a dish towel or paper towel.

2. Make the vinaigrette by putting all the remaining ingredients in a blender and blending on medium speed until the dressing is smooth, about 20 seconds.

3. Transfer the cherry tomatoes to a decorative bowl, pour the dressing over them, and toss gently until they are all lightly coated.

Music

Some Flamenco guitar should get the party off to a lively start. Look for a recording by the Assad Brothers, a dynamic guitar duo, or Otmar Liebert. Then switch to Andre Segovia to calm things down for dinner. After the meal, a tango is definitely in order. Anything by Astor Piazzolla, master of the bandoneon, should do the trick. Make sure to move the furniture in case anyone gets the urge to dance. And have some spare roses handy, in case someone wants one for between their teeth.

Paella Grande

Makes 8 servings

There are as many paellas in Spain as there are cooks. Each has a slight variation, like gumbo in New Orleans or mixed beer nuts in Canton, Ohio. Regional differences have to do with the inclusion of chicken, ham, or seafood. But in all authentic paella, the chicken pieces are included with the bone. If the dish is cooked with boneless chicken, it's called parellade. And it is written that The Inquisition dealt harshly with those who tried to pass off their parellade as paella.

4 cups canned chicken broth, or 4 cups water and 3 chicken bouillon cubes

1 cup bottled clam juice

1 teaspoon saffron

¼ cup warm water

2 tablespoons olive oil

8 chicken thighs

8 chicken drumsticks

2 pounds large shrimp

1 large onion, finely chopped

5 cloves garlic, minced

2⅔ cups converted rice

½ pound chorizo or other spicy smoked sausage

1 package frozen peas, thawed

2 packages frozen artichokes, thawed

One 28-ounce can whole tomatoes, drained

2 roasted red peppers (see page 21), or one 4-ounce jar roasted peppers

1. Preheat the oven to 375°F. Measure the chicken broth (or water and bouillon cubes) and clam juice into a saucepan and heat it slowly over medium heat while you are preparing the ingredients for the paella.

2. Place the saffron in a small bowl and pour the warm water over it. Set aside.

> **TIP**
>
> I found a no-fat smoked turkey sausage in the supermarket that succeeded in giving the paella sufficient of flavor while cutting down on the calories and fat.

3. Heat the olive oil in a large, heavy skillet until it is very hot, about 1½ minutes, spreading the oil so that it evenly glazes the bottom. Add the chicken thighs and cook them until they are brown, about 2 minutes. Turn and cook 2 minutes more. Transfer them to a platter and brown the drumsticks in the same way, transferring them to the platter also when they are done.

4. Add half the shrimp to the hot skillet and cook them, stirring often, until they are pink, about 1 to 1½ minutes. Do not overcook the shrimp because they will finish cooking in the paella. Transfer the cooked shrimp to a platter and cook the remaining shrimp.

5. When you're done with the shrimp, reduce the heat to medium high and add the onion to the pan. Cook until it is soft and translucent, about 4 minutes. Add the garlic and cook 1 minute more. Add the rice and stir until it is lightly coated with oil. Add the water and saffron and stir it into the rice.

6. Transfer the rice to a 12×17-inch baking pan. Add the browned chicken pieces, shrimp, sausage, peas, artichokes, tomatoes, and peppers and stir everything together.

Note

A few dozen mussels and clams traditionally accompany most paellas. If you want to use them, rinse 1 dozen small clams and 1 dozen cultivated mussels in several changes of cold water to get rid of any dirt on their shells. Place them in a large pot with 1 inch of water, cover, and bring the water to a boil. Reduce the heat to medium and steam them for 7 minutes or until their shells are open. Discard any clams or mussels that do not open. It's best to begin steaming them about 45 minutes into the cooking of the paella, so they will be done at the same time. Simply arrange the clams and mussels over the rice before serving.

7. Pour on the hot broth mixture, stir, and cover the pan with aluminum foil. Place the pan in the center rack of the oven and bake for 1 hour or until the rice is cooked through and the chicken has lost its pinkness.

8. When the paella is done, uncover it and serve it in the pan, making sure that you have a substantial trivet on the table.

Mushrooms and Garlic

Makes 8 servings as an appetizer

1 pound medium white mushrooms
3 tablespoons olive oil
4 garlic cloves, minced

Salt and freshly ground black pepper

1. Wipe any dirt from the mushrooms with a lightly damp cloth. Trim the stems to just below the top and set them aside.

2. Heat 2 tablespoons of the olive oil in a large, heavy skillet over medium-high heat until it is very hot, about 1½ minutes, spreading the oil so that it evenly glazes the bottom. Add the mushrooms and cook, stirring often, until they lose their liquid and become soft, about 7 minutes. Add the remaining tablespoon of olive oil and the garlic and cook, stirring continuously, 1 minute more.

3. Season the mushrooms with salt and pepper and transfer them to a bowl to cool. Serve at room temperature in a small serving bowl or platter.

Ice Cream with Tropical Fruit

Makes 8 servings

2 ripe mangoes or papayas
2 ripe kiwis

1 pint strawberries or raspberries
2 pints vanilla ice cream

1. Peel the mangos or papayas. If using mangos, slice the flesh away from the large pit in the middle, and then cut it into 1-inch slices. If using papayas, cut them in half, scoop out the seeds, and cut the flesh into 1-inch slices. Peel the kiwis, cut them in half lengthwise, and then across into ¼-inch, half-moon shaped slices.

2. Rinse the berries. If using strawberries, trim the stems and cut any large berries in half lengthwise.

3. Place two scoops of ice cream in a dessert bowl and arrange the fruit around it.

Sangria

Makes 1 quart

Sadly, in most "Spanish" restaurants in America, the sangria is anything but authentic. Instead of letting the fruit and wine soak together long enough so that their flavors combine, they usually throw some chopped up fruit in a pitcher along with ice, cheap wine, and sugar, creating something that tastes like spiked Kool-ade rather than the classic Andalusian beverage.

1 orange, thinly sliced and seeded

1 lemon, thinly sliced and seeded

1 pint strawberries, stemmed and sliced in half

1 peach, peeled and thinly sliced

1 Granny Smith apple, peeled, cored, and thinly sliced

1 tablespoon sugar

3 tablespoons orange liqueur, such as Cointreau, Grand Marnier, or Triple Sec

3 tablespoons brandy or cognac

1 bottle Spanish red wine, such as a Rioja

8 ice cubes

1. Place all the sliced fruit in a bowl. Sprinkle on the sugar, liqueur, and brandy and toss gently so that all the fruit is coated. Cover and let the fruit macerate (soak in the flavor of the liquor) for 1 to 2 hours in the refrigerator.

2. Transfer the fruit to a large pitcher and add the red wine and ice. Mix together and get out your castanets.

Mr. Pizza Head Kid's Birthday Party

Recipes make 10 servings

Here's a birthday party that combines a kid's three favorite things—pizza, pizza, and pizza. Only this time, instead of ordering in, the kids get to make their own pies, creating pizza faces, or if they're in their abstract period, culinary collages of mozzarella, peppers, and pepperoni never before seen or eaten. And while they're working, they'll learn a little about the history of pizza, the *zeitgeist* of yeast, how mozzarella is made, and why it is important to clean up, especially at someone else's house. This is a great party for eight 5 to 8 year olds. Invite the kids for 11 A.M. or 4 P.M., depending on whether you want a lunch or dinner party, and mention in the invitation that the kids will be making the pizzas, so that no one will wear their really fancy party clothes.

Menu

Carrot and Celery Sticks

Pizza with Pepperoni, Peppers, and Mushrooms

Birthday Cake

Carrot and Celery Sticks

Makes 10 servings as an appetizer

Set these out when the kids arrive. Once they see they pizza, it's unlikely they'll want to eat any vegetables.

1 head celery, rinsed   **2 pounds peeled baby carrots**

1. Cut the celery stalks lengthwise in half and then into 4-inch sticks.

2. Set out the celery with the carrots in decorative bowls on the worktable.

Equipment

36 8-ounce paper cups

Three 11x17-inch baking sheets

Spray oil (to grease aluminum foil)

2 large bowls

Measuring cups

Large cutting board

Large knife or pizza cutter

Roll of heavy brown paper for the table.

Aluminum foil

10 spoons (plastic is okay)

Timetable

Following this schedule will help ensure that everything goes smoothly.

90 minutes before: Make the pizza dough and let it rise.

60 minutes before: Grate the cheese, prepare the toppings, cut up the celery sticks. Cover the table with paper if necessary.

30 minutes before: Fill paper cups with cheese, flour, toppings, and sauce and set on table. Pick out the music you want for the party.

10 minutes before: Preheat the oven to 450°F, and then put the "demonstration yeast" in warm water and a pinch of sugar.

5 minutes before: Meditate.

Pizza

Makes ten 6-inch pizzas

For the dough

5 cups lukewarm water

$\frac{1}{2}$ teaspoon sugar

4 packages dry yeast

$\frac{1}{2}$ cup plus 2 tablespoons olive oil

3 tablespoons salt

14 cups all-purpose flour

For the toppings

3 pounds mozzarella, grated

48 ounces jarred tomato marinara sauce

16 ounces sliced pepperoni, some slices cut into squares and triangles

2 red bell peppers, cut into thin strips

2 green bell peppers, cut into thin strips

2 yellow bell peppers, cut into thin strips

1. Place the water and sugar in a large bowl and sprinkle on the yeast. Let the yeast sit or "proof" for 6 to 8 minutes until it starts to bubble.

Note

See the Fun and Games section, page 232, for tips on organizing, decorating, and baking the pizza.

2. Add the oil and salt. Then add 13 cups of the flour and mix everything together with a large wooden spoon. If the dough is still sticky, add the remaining cup of flour a few tablespoons at a time. Use your hands to finish shaping it into a large soft but not sticky ball.

3. Sprinkle a little flour on your counter and spread it around. Place the dough in the center and knead for a solid 10 minutes until the dough feels smooth and elastic.

4. Lightly coat the inside of a large bowl (you might have to clean out the one you mixed in) with oil and put in the dough. Cover it with a dish towel and place it in a warm, draft-free place to rise. It will be ready to work with in about $1\frac{1}{2}$ hours.

Birthday Cake

Makes 12 to 16 servings

Here's a basic vanilla birthday cake that you can frost and turn into something really fun for your kid. The easiest way to decorate it is to create a scene on top with small plastic figures that coincide with the theme of the party. If it's a baseball party, for example, you could do the top in green icing for the field, run some white lines to make a diamond, and get some toy players to stand around the edge of the field acting either like they're on strike, or their agents want them to hold out for a bigger contract.

3 cups unbleached, all-purpose
   flour
2 teaspoons baking powder
½ teaspoon salt
1 pound (4 sticks) butter

2½ cups sugar
8 large eggs, separated
2 tablespoons vanilla
Easy Butter Frosting (recipe
   follows)

1. Preheat the oven to 325°F. Generously grease two 9x12-inch baking pans or aluminum lasagna pans, line the bottom with wax paper, and lightly grease the wax paper. In a medium mixing bowl, stir together the flour, baking powder and salt with a whisk until they are well combined.

2. In a large mixing bowl, cream together the butter and sugar with an electric mixer on medium speed until the mixture is smooth and pale yellow, about 3 minutes. Add the egg yolks one at a time, beating well after each one. Add the vanilla and continue beating until just combined. Add the flour mixture and beat until just combined.

3. Clean the beaters well and beat the egg whites until they are light and frothy. Use a rubber spatula to gently fold the egg whites into the batter. Do this by stirring slowly out from the center until all the egg whites are combined into the batter.

Note

You will probably want to bake and decorate the cake the night before the party. The best way to store it is to buy a large rectangular cake box from a local bakery, set the cake inside, and refrigerate. You also can improvise storage from a suitably sized cardboard box, which you might have to cut down to fit in the fridge. Remove the cake from the refrigerator 1 hour before serving.

4. Transfer half the batter to each of the baking pans and bake on the center rack of the oven for 30 to 35 minutes or until a toothpick inserted in the center comes out clean. Let the cake cool for 20 minutes before removing from the pan. Let cool another 45 minutes before decorating. Now you are ready to decorate the cake.

5. Prepare the frosting (recipe follows).

6. Place one layer on a decorative platter. Top with a thin, even layer of frosting. Place the second cake on top of the first. Use a serrated knife to trim the sides to make even edges all around. Also trim the top a bit to flatten it out. Spread a thin, even layer of frosting over the whole cake. Use store-bought colored tubes of frosting to decorate the top or add food coloring to leftover frosting, spoon it into a small squeeze bottle, and use that for decoration. Add small plastic figures for additional effects.

Music

Once kids reach 5 years old, they get particular about their music, so you should definitely consult the birthday kid about what kind of music he or she wants. A fun activity would be to spend an evening putting together a tape of your child's favorite songs to play at the party. Then if you have a double cassette player, you can dub copies of the birthday tape and give one to each guest in their party bag.

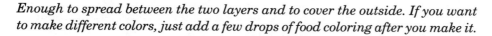

Easy Butter Frosting

Enough to spread between the two layers and to cover the outside. If you want to make different colors, just add a few drops of food coloring after you make it.

¾ cup (1½ sticks) butter at room temperature

½ cup plus 1 tablespoon milk

1 tablespoon vanilla

5 cups confectioner's sugar, plus additional cup if needed

1. In a large bowl, cream the butter with an electric beater on medium speed until it is light and fluffy.

2. Add the milk, vanilla, and 5 cups of the confectioner's sugar and continue mixing until the mixture is well combined. Add additional confectioner's sugar ¼ cup at a time until the frosting reaches a spreadable consistency.

Note

To turn this into a chocolate frosting, add 6 ounces melted and slightly cooled semisweet chocolate to the butter before beating.

Fun and Games

This whole party is fun and games. Here are some helpful pointers to guide you through.

When throwing a kid's party, it's absolutely crucial that everything be ready the moment the kids arrive. Otherwise, they start wandering around your house looking for shoeboxes of baseball cards or other keepsakes they can rifle for their own collections. With this factor in mind, make sure that you start the dough about 90 minutes before liftoff so that it has a chance to rise. And while the dough is rising, you can grate the cheese and cut the peppers and pepperoni so that they are ready for the little bakers when they arrive.

After all the food prep is done, set up the table. Try removing the chairs and have the kids stand to make their pizzas. This gives them more room and better leverage for shaping the dough. If you're worried about the finish of the table, you can cover it widthwise with heavy brown wrapping paper secured underneath with masking tape.

Using 8-ounce paper cups is the perfect way to distribute the ingredients for each kid. Every kid should get one cup each of the following: about ¼ cup of flour, 6 ounces of sauce, and 6 ounces of grated cheese. Set them at each kid's workstation along with a 12-inch square sheet of lightly oiled aluminum foil and a spoon. Place an assortment of peppers and pepperoni on several dinner plates and put them on the table. And be sure to preheat the oven to 450°F. Nothing could be worse than having all the pizzas ready and not being able to bake them off.

Dad's Pizza Speech

Pizza is a traditional Italian dish, which some people believe originated in New Jersey but really came from Naples, a large island just off the coast of Italy. The ingredients for the dough are flour, yeast, olive oil, and salt. The basic toppings are tomato sauce and mozzarella cheese, and can include ones we know, like sausage, pepperoni, mushrooms, and peppers. And more exotic ones, like anchovies, raw eggs, squid, pineapple, and octopus.

As soon as the kids arrive, have them wash their hands, letting them know it's what you always do before working with food. Direct them to their places and bring out the bowl of dough for them to see and feel while you tell them a little bit about pizza.

Shaping the Dough

Have the kids sprinkle a tablespoon of flour on the table in front of them and rub it around to make a thin, white coating the size of a pie plate to keep the dough from sticking. The big ball of dough now needs to be punched down. This is the special responsibility of the birthday child, who gets to left jab and right hook it into submission. Each child should then tear off a softball-size piece of dough to work with.

The kids should knead the dough for a couple of minutes. Then have them place the dough on their square of aluminum foil and give it a 3-minute nap to restore its elasticity. This would be an opportune time to bring around the bowl of demonstration yeast.

Making the Pizzas

After the dough has rested for a few minutes, the kids are ready to shape their pizzas. They should use their fingertips to push out from the center to shape the dough into a rough circle about 8 inches across. Some of the kids will create more imaginative shapes resembling amoebas or the paisley designs on vintage neckties. This is perfectly fine and makes identifying them later that much easier. They also can make funny pizza faces, using some pepperoni for the eyes, yellow pepper for the nose, and red pepper for the mouth.

Next comes the sauce, which should be poured out in the center of the dough in a circle about the size of, as one of our guests put it, a "half a baseball, squashed." Have them use the backs of their spoons to spread the sauce in an even layer over the dough. Beware of sauce overload—which makes for runny, soggy, hard-to-eat pizzas.

Next, instruct the kids to sprinkle on the cheese—as little or as much as they want. Then, encourage the kids to create designs with the peppers and pepperoni. They also can shape their initials with the pepper sticks.

Baking

Place the pizzas and their foil on a baking sheet, 4 per sheet. Slip the pans in the oven and close it quickly to keep in the heat. If you used two racks, you'll

Dad's Yeast Speech

It's alive! Yes, even though it looks like sand, yeast is actually made up of microscopic organisms, which is a fancy way of saying that they are really, really tiny. And like other living things, the tiny yeast organisms like to eat and drink. So if you put the yeast in water that's not too cold and not too hot, just like a bath, and give it a little sugar to eat, it gets very happy and gorges itself. Also, like other living things, if it eats too much, it passes gas. These are the bubbles that form on the surface of the water. It also smells. These bubbles are what help make the dough light and fluffy. The heat of the oven kills the yeast when the pizza is baking. Except if it's Super Yeast, which can't be killed and lives inside your socks.

need to rotate the pans between the higher and lower racks after 7 minutes of baking. Check after 12 minutes to see whether they are done. The crusts should be light brown on the bottom and the cheese should be melted completely. If you can't get them all baked at once, have a few kids in the first wave share with those in the second.

While the pizzas are baking, the kids can help clean the table. And when they're done with that, they can work on the garage. We also passed out packs of baseball, novelty, and superhero cards, which kept most of the boys and girls occupied while the pizzas were in the oven. A few chose to help set the table for lunch, which required distributing napkins and cups, along with the platters of carrots and celery sticks. The plates should be stacked in the kitchen, ready to receive the pizzas.

Serving

Place a trivet or a few dishcloths on the counter to receive the hot pans. Remove the pans and place them on the counter. Use a large spatula to transfer the pizzas from the foil to the cutting board. Cut them into quarters, slip them onto a plate, and distribute to their creators. Make sure to warn the kids about letting the pizzas cool a bit before eating them to avoid the dreaded "pizza burn."

The Big Picture

Here's an activity that should keep the kids occupied for a while. Tape about 12 feet of the brown paper on to the floor and let the kids create a collective mural. Give them crayons, colored pencils, and a large assortment of stickers and let them gather along the paper and make art to their hearts' content. You can give them a theme or not. They can also write their names so the birthday boy or girl will remember who was at the party.

Saturday Night Chili Party

Recipes make 12 servings

Everyone knows what they're getting into when you're serving chili. It's about dressing casual, dancing to good music, whoopin' and hollerin', and having a good ol' time.

One of the reasons the guests can enjoy themselves so much is because you, the host, are exceptionally laid back. Even though there's quite a crowd coursing through your living room, tapping on the glass of the fish tank, checking out the tile job you did in the front hallway, fingering the four-foot souvenir spoon and fork hanging on the wall that you got on that trip to Mexico, you feel at ease. You've got the Big Pot on the stove and it's filled with chili and all you've got to do is put it on the table with a ladle and some bowls and you're golden. It's like the feeling of having the winner of the top half of the Daily Double coupled with every horse in the second race—whatever happens, you win.

Making chili is labor intensive but not overly challenging—like building something out of Legos. Set aside an hour and enjoy yourself. Put the ball game or Car Talk on the radio, or throw in a cassette of Jack Kerouac doing his literary-jazz-jam-session thing and make it fun.

MENU

Sangritas
Salsa and Chips
Texas Chili
Cornbread
Brown Rice
Romaine, Corn, and Black Bean Salad
with Avocado Dressing
Blueberry Pear Cobbler

Sangritas

Makes 12 servings

At Zarela, one of my favorite Mexican restaurants in New York, they sometimes serve a drink called a sangrita, which is a mysterious concoction of pomegranate juice accompanied by a shot of tequila. Unable to pry the exact recipe for Zarela and knowing that even if I did, there aren't many places you can run out and pick up a six-pack of pomegranate juice, I gave up hope. Then I heard about sangrita a friend of a friend had created, made, she swore, with tomato juice, orange juice, and lime juice. I experimented and... well, here it is. It's not for the faint of heart, but then few good things are.

½ cup tomato juice

⅓ cup orange juice

½ cup fresh lime juice

2 dashes Tabasco

2 limes, cut into quarters

1 fifth of tequila

1. Mix the tomato juice, orange juice, lime juice, and Tabasco in a small pitcher and chill.

2. To serve, pour an ounce or so of tequila into a shot glass or cordial glass. Pour the same amount of the sangrita mixture into another glass. Drink a sip of the tequila, then the sangrita, and then suck hard on the lime.

Music

There are two ways to go here. You can play some Texas Swing, such as a few Bob Wills or Commander Cody discs, or a current CD called *Roy Rogers Tribute* to give the party a loping, jaunty feeling. Also Rhino Records has a 3-CD set called *Songs of the West*, which will make you feel like you're sitting around the campfire. Or something more south of the border, like Los Lobos. ZZ Top and Stevie Ray Vaughn are both Texas rockers who could spice up the party. For something in between, check out Steve Turre, a jazz trombone and shell player whose music has a great Latin feel, especially his album *Rhythm Within*.

Salsa and Chips

Makes 12 servings as an appetizer

I made this on the mild side. If you like your salsa hotter, you can add more jalapeños and make it as caliente as you want.

8 ripe plum tomatoes, cut length-wise into quarters

1 red bell pepper, cored, seeded, and cut into quarters

1 green bell pepper, cored, seeded, and cut into quarters

1 small red onion, peeled and cut into quarters

3 cloves garlic, coarsely chopped

¼ cup cilantro leaves

2 tablespoons fresh lime juice

1 tablespoon chili powder

1 teaspoon salt

1 teaspoon canned jalapeños, chopped

½ teaspoon ground cumin

1-pound bag of tortilla chips

1. Place all the ingredients except the chips in the bowl of a food processor fitted with a steel blade.

2. Pulse until all the ingredients are finely chopped, about 12 pulses.

3. Transfer to a serving bowl and serve with tortilla chips.

Note

If you don't have a food processor, chop the tomatoes, peppers, onion, and garlic separately and as finely as possible. Transfer them to a mixing bowl and stir in the rest of the ingredients.

Texas Chili

Makes 12 servings

What distinguishes Texas-style chili from the others is the use of chunks of meat rather than ground beef. To me, this gives the chili a less voluble texture and consistency.

5 strips bacon

5 red bell peppers, stemmed, seeded, and cut into 1-inch pieces

2 large onions, coarsely chopped

4 cloves garlic, finely chopped

2 tablespoons vegetable oil

4 pounds beef stew, cut into 1-inch pieces

½ cup mild chili powder

One 28-ounce can crushed tomatoes

5 cups canned beef broth

1 ounce canned jalapeños, chopped

Three 16-ounce cans red beans

Hot, cooked brown rice for serving (see page 243)

Note

Note: If you buy meat that already has been cut for stew, the pieces might be a bit large for chili. Try cutting the larger pieces in half so that they are closer to 1 inch.

Chili can be made the day before it is served. A night in the refrigerator only enhances its flavor. Let the chili cool before refrigerating it right in the pot. Reheat it slowly, stirring frequently, over a medium-low heat so that the chili on the bottom is not scorched.

1. Place a large, heavy-bottomed pot over medium-high heat and let it get hot, about 1½ minutes. Add the bacon and cook until it is crisp, about 5 minutes. Remove the bacon with a slotted spoon and transfer it to some paper towels. Pour off all but 2 tablespoons of the bacon fat from the pot, add the onions and peppers, and cook, stirring often, until soft, about 10 minutes. Add the garlic and cook 2 minutes more. Transfer the vegetables to a large bowl and set aside.

2. Return the pot to the heat and add 1 tablespoon of the oil and half the meat. Cook, stirring often, until it is lightly brown, about 4 minutes. Transfer the meat to the bowl with the vegetables and brown the remaining meat. Add the chili powder and cook, stirring continuously, for 1 minute.

3. Return the vegetables and first batch of meat to the pot along with the tomatoes, broth, and jalapeños and bring the mixture to a boil, stirring often. Reduce the heat to medium low and cook, partially covered, for 1½ hours, stirring occasionally. Remove the cover and cook 30 minutes more, stirring occasionally. Add the beans and the bacon strips cut into small pieces and cook 15 minutes more, stirring occasionally. Serve hot with rice and toppings.

Toppings

Serve the chili accompanied by bowls of the following:

Grated sharp Cheddar or Monterey Jack cheese

Finely chopped red onion

Sour cream

Cornbread

Makes 12 servings

This is cornbread with a little sweetness to it. That's the way I like it.

2½ cups all-purpose, unbleached
   flour
1½ cups yellow cornmeal
½ cup sugar
5 teaspoons baking powder

1 teaspoon salt
2 cups milk
2 eggs
½ cup (1 stick) butter, melted

1. Preheat the oven to 375°F. Butter a 9x16-inch baking pan. In a large bowl, use a whisk to stir together the flour, cornmeal, sugar, baking powder, and salt.

2. In a medium bowl, use a whisk to mix together the milk, eggs, and melted butter. Pour the wet ingredients into the dry ingredients and stir with a wooden spoon until they are just combined. Be sure to stir right down to the bottom. Use a rubber spatula to transfer the batter into the prepared pan. Smooth out the top and bake on the center rack until it is lightly brown and a toothpick inserted in the center comes out clean, about 22 minutes. Let the cornbread cool before cutting it into pieces.

drinks

Beer is what to drink at this party—Newman to your chili's Redford. Lone Star or Dos Equis are two brands often served with spicy foods. However, you might want to use this meal as an impetus to try some of the beer now being made by microbreweries all around the country. Find out what's being brewed near you and maybe sample a few different brands. For the kids, whip up a batch of lemonade from the recipe on page 146.

Brown Rice

Makes 12 servings

I like to serve brown rice instead of white rice with this meal because its heartier flavor stands up to the chili. You also can use a combination of wild rice or Wehani rice along with the brown. Feel free to mix them together as they all have the same cooking time. Unlike white rice, brown rice is put in the pot at the same time as the water. Be sure not to forget to lower the heat when it comes to a boil.

6 cups water
3 cups long grain brown rice

2 tablespoons butter

1. Measure the water, rice, and butter into a medium saucepan and bring the water to a boil.

2. Immediately reduce the heat to low, cover the pan, and cook the rice at a low simmer for 50 to 55 minutes until the water is absorbed and the rice is just cooked through. Be sure not to lift the cover until close to the end of the cooking time when you're checking to see if the rice is done.

3. Fluff with a fork just before serving.

Romaine, Corn, and Black Bean Salad with Avocado Dressing

Makes 12 servings

*A **nifty**, Southwestern-style salad that looks pretty and is easy to make. Show it off at the table before tossing with the dressing.*

2 heads Romaine lettuce, washed and cut into 2-inch pieces

One 16-ounce can black beans

6 ears of corn, cooked, with the kernels cut off; or two 12-ounce cans corn packed in water

1 small red onion, thinly sliced

2 endives, cut into ½-inch slices

1 red bell pepper, stemmed, seeded, and cut into ½-inch pieces

For the dressing

1 ripe avocado

1 cup plain yogurt

2 tablespoons fresh lime juice

2 whole scallions, cut into 1-inch pieces

½ teaspoon salt

A dash Tabasco

1. Place the Romaine in a large salad bowl. Empty the black beans into a strainer and rinse them briefly with cold water. Scatter the beans, along with the corn, red onion, endive, and red pepper, over the lettuce.

2. Place all the ingredients for the dressing in the bowl of a food processor and pulse until the mixture is smooth, about 10 pulses. If you don't have a food processor, use a potato masher to mash the avocado, yogurt, and lime juice as smoothly as possible. Chop the scallions very fine and stir them in along with the salt and Tabasco.

3. Just before serving, pour the dressing over the salad and toss well.

Blueberry Pear Cobbler

Makes 16 servings

I was in Atlanta once and my host, knowing that I loved down-home cooking, promised to take me for what she swore would be the best fried chicken and dumplings I'd ever had. They were served in a hole-in-the-wall luncheonette just outside of town. After blindfolding me and making me lie down in the backseat to keep me from broadcasting the whereabouts of this local treasure, thus protecting the delicate fried chicken ecosystem, she led me to a very unassuming dive, where I had a plate of chicken every bit as good as she said it would be. For dessert, they served up a cobbler (from a pan the size of a small pool table) that very much resembled this one. Because it was Georgia, theirs was made with peaches they had poached and put up in jars earlier in the year. Knowing that it's not always easy to find fresh peaches, I've worked this one up for pears and blueberries.

6 Bartlet pears

4 pints fresh or frozen blueberries

1 cup all-purpose, unbleached flour

2½ cups oats

⅔ cup brown sugar

2 cups walnuts, coarsely chopped

2 teaspoons cinnamon

¾ cup (1½ sticks) butter at room temperature

1. Preheat the oven to 350°F. Butter two 9x12-inch lasagna pans (aluminum is fine). Cut the pears lengthwise into quarters and trim away the core from each section. Cut each section across into 3 pieces. Transfer the pear pieces to a large mixing bowl along with the blueberries. Sprinkle on ½ cup of flour and mix so that the fruit is lightly dusted. Transfer the fruit equally to the 2 prepared pans.

2. In a medium mixing bowl, combine the oats, remaining ½ cup of flour, brown sugar, walnuts, and cinnamon and stir until combined. Add the butter and stir until it is incorporated into the oat mixture. You might have to use your fingers for the final stage of this. Sprinkle the mixture over the top of the fruit in an even layer. Don't worry if you miss a few spots.

3. Bake on the center rack of the oven until the crust turns light brown, about 35 minutes. Let the cobbler cool for 20 minutes before serving.

Note

The cobbler is best served the day it is made, and because it's so easy to prepare, that shouldn't be hard to do. If you make it earlier in the day, don't cover it with plastic wrap because it will make the cobbler crust soggy. Instead, drape a clean cloth or paper towel over the pan and leave it at room temperature.

Like any cobbler, this one is best served warm with some vanilla ice cream.

Thanksgiving

Recipes make 16 servings

The pressure's on here. It's put up or shut up. The prefight hype is over, now it's time to get in the culinary ring. The relatives are coming your way for the Meal of the Year, and it had better be good. You bought this cookbook and you've been bragging, and rightfully so. But very soon The Thanksgiving Crowd will descend on your table—your relatives, like the First Cavalry in *Apocalypse Now,* choppers roaring, *Ride of the Valykres* blaring, *Death from Above,* they'll be chewing with their mouths open, spilling grape juice on the tablecloth, grinding gravy into the rug, and expecting something spectacular to eat.

Despite the onslaught, you're going to impress them anyway, even though you know your aunt will make some kind of remark about the sausage in the stuffing—that it's not the way *she* makes stuffing. Or that Cousin Susan likes to do something *else* with the sweet potatoes. They're basically nice people, and once they grasp the idea that you're a better cook, they'll hopefully be civil about it.

MeNU
Cranberry Biscuits
Turkey with Turkey Sausage Stuffing
Yams with Apples
Pear and Cranberry Sauce
String Bean and Corn Succotash
Apple Cake
Hot Mulled Cider

Cranberry Biscuits

Makes 16 biscuits

The thing about hot biscuits—just out of the oven and broken in half with butter melting and oozing through the crevices—is that they make people happy. Biscuit-baking moms have known this for a long time. Now it's time for dad to get in on some of this action.

2 cups unbleached, all-purpose flour

1 tablespoon baking powder

1 teaspoon salt

6 tablespoons Crisco shortening

1 beaten large egg plus enough milk to make ¾ cup liquid

2 tablespoons butter

2 tablespoons honey

6 ounces fresh cranberries

1. Preheat the oven to 425°F and lightly grease a cookie sheet. In a large bowl, use a whisk to stir together the flour, baking powder, and salt. Add the shortening to the flour mixture and use your fingertips to break it up into small, pea-sized bits.

2. Beat the egg in a small bowl and transfer it to a measuring cup along with enough milk to make ¾ cup. Pour it into the flour mixture and use a wooden spoon to stir it into a soft dough. Sprinkle some flour on the counter and knead the dough until it is smooth, about 3 minutes. (See page 86 for kneading tips.)

3. Sprinkle more flour on the counter and use a rolling pin to roll out the dough about ½ inch thick. Use a cookie cutter to cut out the biscuits or simply cut them roughly into 16 squares and place them on the cookie sheet about 1 inch apart.

Note

You can prepare the biscuits through step 3 up to 8 hours in advance. Simply cover the cookie sheet lightly with plastic wrap and store the biscuits in the refrigerator.

4. Place the butter and honey in a small saucepan over low heat and cook until the butter is melted, about 1 minute. This also can be done in the microwave on a medium setting for about 15 seconds. Use a pastry brush to brush the tops of the biscuits with the butter mixture. Arrange 3 or 4 cranberries on top of the biscuits, pressing them down very slightly into the dough.

5. Bake on the center rack for 12 to 14 minutes or until the biscuits are lightly brown.

Roast Turkey

Makes 16 servings

Make sure that you remember to get the stuffing ready before you're ready to put the bird in the oven. Also, it's very important that you remember to remove the neck stuffed inside the big cavity in the front and the little bag of gizzards from the cavity in the rear. One of the raps against us men doing the cooking is that we do things like cook the turkey with the gizzards still inside. You don't want the women folk using that as fodder to mock us during their mahjong games.

One 18- to 20-pound turkey, neck and giblets removed

1 orange, cut in half

6 cups turkey sausage stuffing (recipe follows)

¾ pound bacon or turkey bacon

1. Preheat the oven to 350°F. Rinse the inside of the turkey under cold running water and shake out the excess water. Rub the inside of the cavity with half an orange, squeezing the orange so that the juice coats the cavity. Place the turkey in a large, sturdy roasting pan (aluminum is okay). Use a large mixing spoon or your hands to fill the main cavity and the rear one with stuffing. Lay the strips of bacon over the breast of the turkey in an even layer. Cover the pan loosely with aluminum foil.

2. Bake the turkey for 18 minutes per pound. After the first 2 hours, remove the foil. After another hour, remove the bacon. When there is enough juice in the bottom of the pan, tip the pan slightly and use a turkey baster to baste the turkey.

3. When the turkey is done, remove it from the oven and let it cool for 10 minutes before slicing. Baste every 45 minutes during the last 3 hours of cooking.

drinks

Thanksgiving dinner is not usually associated with drinking wine. Because the meal generally segues into a football game on TV, sipping a glass of fine Bordeaux seems a little *parvenu*. If you care for wine during the meal, a soft, fruity red such as a Beaujolais, Portuguese Rosé, or California White Zinfandel probably would be in order. I enjoy a dark ale or stout with my turkey and trimmings. The kids might like sparkling cider as a special treat during the meal.

Turkey Sausage Stuffing

Makes 6 cups

1 tablespoon butter

1 medium onion, finely chopped

2 celery stalks, coarsely chopped

2 cloves garlic, finely chopped

¾ pound turkey sausage meat

1 cup sherry

1 bouillon cube

4 cups white, wheat, or oatmeal
bread, cut into ½-inch cubes

½ cup raisins

½ cup cream or milk

½ teaspoon dried thyme

½ teaspoon salt

Freshly ground black pepper

Note

To get the sausage meat, simply slice open the sausage casings and scrape out the meat. Or you can squeeze it out as you would toothpaste.

1. Place a large frying pan over medium-high heat. Add the butter to the pan and, as it starts sizzling, spread it so that it evenly glazes the bottom. Add the onions and celery and cook, stirring frequently, until they soften, about 6 minutes. Add the garlic and cook 1 minute more. Transfer the onion mixture to a large mixing bowl and wipe out the pan.

2. Return the pan to the stove and increase the heat to high. Add the sausage meat and cook, stirring continuously, until it loses its pinkness, about 3 minutes. Break up the sausage meat as best you can while it is cooking. Add the sherry and bouillon cube to the pan and stir to dissolve the bouillon and to scrape up any pieces of sausage stuck to the bottom of the pan. When the bouillon is dissolved, transfer the sausage mixture to the bowl with the onions. Add the rest of the ingredients and mix together with a large spoon or your fingers until well combined.

Yams and Apples

Makes 16 servings

A Thanksgiving favorite. Or if it's not, it will be.

10 medium yams, peeled

4 tart apples, such Granny Smith
or Gala, peeled

6 tablespoons butter

1½ cups milk

½ cup brown sugar

¼ cup molasses

1 egg

2 teaspoons fresh lemon juice

2 teaspoons cinnamon

2 teaspoons salt

1 cup mini marshmallows
(optional)

½ teaspoon nutmeg

1. Cut the peeled yams into ½-inch circles and place them in a large pot with enough water to cover them. Bring the water to a boil over high heat, and then reduce the heat to medium and simmer the yams until they are soft, about 20 minutes.

2. While the yams are boiling, cut the apples into quarters and trim the core from each quarter. Place a large frying pan over medium-high heat. Add 2 tablespoons of the butter to the pan and, as it starts sizzling, spread it so that it evenly glazes the bottom. Add the apple slices and cook, stirring frequently until they turn slightly brown, about 6 minutes. Turn off the heat and set aside.

3. When the potatoes are cooked through, drain them in a colander and then return them to the pot. Add the milk, the remaining 4 tablespoons of butter, sugar, molasses, egg, lemon juice, cinnamon, salt, and nutmeg and beat with an electric mixer on medium speed until the mixture is smooth, about 3 minutes. If you don't have an electric mixer, use a potato masher.

Note

Because there may be a turkey in the oven, you may not be able to fit the potatoes on one of the racks. One solution might be to ask a neighbor if you can use their oven. Or you often can find a way to rest the sweet potatoes on the edge of the turkey pan. As long as it's in the oven and you can get the door closed, it will be all right.

Kids sometimes like tiny marshmallows over their sweet potatoes. You might want to scatter a few over one half the pan for the last 10 minutes of baking.

4. Preheat the oven to 350°F. Lightly grease a 12×19-inch baking pan. Transfer the sweet potatoes to the baking pan and smooth the top. Arrange the apple slices in two neat rows down the pan. Cover the pan with aluminum foil and bake for 30 minutes. Remove the foil and bake 10 minutes more.

Pear and Cranberry Sauce

Makes 2 pints

The perfect accompaniment for your turkey.

3 pears

Two 12-ounce bags fresh cranberries

½ cup brown sugar

½ cup white sugar

1 cup orange juice, preferably fresh

Grated zest of 1 orange

Note

You can make the cranberry sauce up to 2 days in advance. Store in the refrigerator in a well-sealed plastic container.

1. Cut the pears lengthwise into quarters. Trim the core from each quarter, cut them in half lengthwise, and then cut them across into thirds.

2. Place the pears, along with the rest of the ingredients, into a medium saucepan over medium-high heat. Bring the liquid to a boil, and then immediately reduce the heat to medium low and simmer, stirring frequently with the pan uncovered, until the mixture thickens and the cranberries begin to pop, about 8 minutes.

3. Transfer the sauce to a serving bowl and let the mixture cool before refrigerating.

String Bean and Corn Succotash

Makes 16 servings

This is not "sufferin' succotash" but a cool and eponymous way to present the Thanksgiving vegetables.

2 tablespoons butter

1 small onion, finely chopped

1 red bell pepper, cored, seeded, and cut into large dice

¼ pound smoked ham, cut into ½-inch cubes

2 pounds string beans, washed, stemmed, and cut into 1-inch pieces

6 ears fresh corn cut off the cob, or one 16-ounce bag frozen corn

1 cup canned chicken broth

1 teaspoon sugar

Salt and freshly ground black pepper

1. Place a large frying pan over medium-high heat. Add the butter to the pan and, as it starts sizzling, spread it so that it evenly glazes the bottom. Add the onion and red pepper and cook, stirring frequently, until they just get soft, about 4 minutes. Add the ham and cook, stirring continuously, until the ham is heated through, about 1 minute.

2. Add the string beans, corn, chicken broth, and sugar and bring the liquid to a boil. As soon as it boils, cover the pan and reduce the heat to medium low. Cook the succotash until the beans and corn are cooked through, about 8 minutes. Serve immediately.

Note

Have the deli person cut you one slice of smoked ham about ½-inch thick, which should be just right for this recipe. If it's a little over, either use the extra or save it for omelets.

You can make succotash up to 1 hour before serving. Let it sit at room temperature and reheat over low heat just before serving.

Apple Cake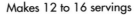

Makes 12 to 16 servings

After everyone has this cake, you'll be asked to make it for every Thanksgiving, whether you're doing the rest of the meal or not. It will become your family's Thanksgiving mantra—"Oh, and of course Fred will make the cake."

4 tart apples, such as Granny Smith or Gala, peeled

2 tablespoons fresh lemon juice

2 cups plus 3 tablespoons sugar

1 tablespoon cinnamon

2½ cups all-purpose, unbleached flour

1 tablespoon baking powder

1 cup (2 sticks) butter, at room temperature

2 eggs

1 cup sour cream

¼ cup orange juice

1 teaspoon vanilla

1. Preheat the oven to 325°F. Lightly grease a 9½-inch bundt pan. Cut the apples into quarters and cut the core from each quarter. Cut each quarter across into 4 pieces and put them in a large mixing bowl. Add the lemon juice and sprinkle on the 3 tablespoons of sugar and the cinnamon. Toss gently so that all the apple pieces are lightly coated and set aside.

2. In a medium mixing bowl, stir together the flour and baking powder with a whisk until they are well combined.

3. In a large mixing bowl, cream together the butter and the remaining sugar with an electric mixer on medium speed or with a wooden spoon until the mixture is smooth, about 2 minutes. Add the eggs one at a time and stir until well combined. Add the sour cream, orange juice, and vanilla and stir until well combined.

Note

You can make the cake the day before you serve it. After removing it from the pan, let it cool completely before transferring it to a plate and covering it well with plastic. You also can make this cake up to two weeks in advance and freeze it, making sure that you wrap it in the same manner.

4. Stir the flour mixture into the butter mixture until it is just combined. Use a rubber spatula to transfer half the batter into the prepared pan. Arrange half the apples over the batter and cover with the remaining batter. Arrange the remaining apples on top. Bake on the center rack for 1½ hours, or until a toothpick inserted in the center comes out clean. Let the cake cool for 20 minutes on a cake rack. Then invert the pan to remove the cake and let it cool for another 30 minutes before serving.

Hot Mulled Cider

Makes 8 to 10 servings

After the meal, the kids may want to run around outside for a while. When they come in, you can hit them with a cup of hot mulled cider to warm them up.

½ **gallon apple cider**

¾ **cup brown sugar**

¼ **cup fresh lemon juice (2 lemons)**

2 **cinnamon sticks**

½ **teaspoon nutmeg**

½ **teaspoon ground ginger**

2 **oranges, thinly sliced**

Place all ingredients in a large saucepan over medium-low heat and bring to a simmer, stirring occasionally. Serve hot in a mug.

Music

Thanksgiving lends itself to music that different generations can sing along to—folk music such as The Weavers, Leadbelly, and Woody Guthrie might get everyone singing along. You also could try some Simon and Garfunkle, Bob Dylan, Lovin' Spoonful, or Joan Baez. After dinner, the comedy songs of Allen Sherman, Stan Freberg, or Tom Lehrer might send everyone home laughing. Of course, if, like my family, everyone eats a little more than they should, you might want to put a Richard Simmons tape in the VCR and get everyone sweatin' to the oldies.

Tailgating in the Rumpus —A Football Lunch

Recipes make 8 servings

It's Sunday. Game day. And there's a lot to do.

First, you have to find the remote. Then you can tune in to get caught up on the college scores from Saturday, which usually include a string of upsets that seem to confound the announcers terribly, throwing them into a state of deep anxiety and fracturing their sense of the cosmos. After the college report, there's the initial NFL pregame show, which prepares you for what's ahead later on the actual pregame show. Then, finally, following the pregame report, it's time for football. Two games in the afternoon, another in the evening, and at least one postgame report so that you can see again in close-up slow motion the best catches, runs, and hits of the day. After nine hours plus of football and related reporting, it's finally time to grab your blankie and curl up in your crib, exhausted from another strenuous Sunday.

But man does not live by football alone. At some point, you've got to eat. And for this Sunday at least, you and your friends are going to eat well.

Anyone—even the most dedicated football fan—can get it together to make a few sub sandwiches and supplement those with chips, slaw, a bag of cookies, and some beer and/or pop. This might be good enough for the regular season, but for the playoffs, you probably want something special, so that the spread (food) is as important as the spread (points). To this end, there is this brisket, which marinates overnight and then cooks slowly, so that it radiates barbecue. Then it's sliced and arranged on soft French bread, the sauce soaks in, and suddenly

MᴇNU

Barbecue Brisket Sandwiches
Coleslaw
Fried New Potatoes
Banana Splits with Cognac Hot Fudge

you start seeing the game from a different perspective; it becomes almost incidental, no longer a contest between valiant warriors but just a reason to have lunch. The only foreseeable problem is that after this meal, your buddies might not want to watch the game anywhere else. They might not even want to eat anywhere else.

Barbecue Brisket Sandwiches

Makes 8 hearty sandwiches

These are the Johnny Unitas of sandwiches. There's nothing casual about them. The flavor leaps out at you and keeps coming. One sandwich probably won't be enough, so be prepared to run into the kitchen during a time-out to make a few more. The bread should be slathered in sauce, so it's not necessarily a neat meal. Have plenty of napkins on hand. The brisket requires 4 hours in the oven, so you'll have to get started early.

1 cup ketchup

3 tablespoons Worcestershire sauce

1 tablespoon brown sugar

1 tablespoon chili powder

1 teaspoon Dijon mustard

1 teaspoon liquid smoke

1 teaspoon garlic powder

4 dashes Tabasco

2 large onions, peeled, trimmed, cut in half lengthwise, and then into thin slices

4 cloves garlic, peeled and coarsely chopped

2 cups barbecue sauce (recipe follows)

1. Preheat the oven to 325°F. In a medium bowl, mix together the ketchup, Worcestershire sauce, brown sugar, chili powder, mustard, liquid smoke, garlic powder, and Tabasco sauce until well combined.

2. Place the brisket in a 12x18-inch roasting pan and spread the sauce over the top. Arrange the onions and garlic around the edges of the pan. Cover with aluminum foil and bake on the center rack for 4 hours.

3. Remove the pan from the oven and let the brisket cool for 30 minutes. Transfer the brisket to a cutting board and slice it across the grain into the thinnest slices you can.

4. Arrange several slices over a section of French bread. Top with barbecue sauce and serve with more sauce on the side.

drinks

Beer. Cold. Numerous.

Barbecue Sauce

Makes 2 cups

Men can develop specific taste in their barbecue sauce, the way they do for their putter. This one is a good basic sauce. Not quite like the one at Goode and Co., in Houston, but it will do. Feel free to adapt to suit your own taste.

1 cup jarred medium-hot salsa

1 cup chili sauce

1 medium onion, peeled and coarsely chopped

2 tablespoons olive oil

2 cloves garlic

2 teaspoons mild chili powder

2 tablespoons brown sugar

1 tablespoon lemon juice

$\frac{1}{2}$ teaspoon canned jalapeño peppers

$\frac{1}{2}$ teaspoon liquid smoke

1. Put all the ingredients into a blender and puree until the mixture is smooth, about 20 seconds.

2. Transfer the pureed mixture to a medium saucepan and bring to a simmer over medium-low heat. Simmer the sauce partially covered for 20 minutes, stirring occasionally.

3. Let the sauce cool to room temperature before serving.

Coleslaw

Makes 8 servings

This is not the sloppy coleslaw you get at most deli counters, but something more flavorful and sublime.

½ **medium head cabbage (about 2 pounds)**

2 **carrots, peeled and grated**

1 **small red onion, peeled and grated**

2 **tablespoons mayonnaise**

2 **tablespoons sour cream**

1 **tablespoon white wine vinegar**

1 **tablespoon vegetable oil**

1 **teaspoon salt**

1 **teaspoon sugar**

½ **teaspoon celery seed (optional)**

1. Cut the half cabbage in half through the core, and then trim the core from each piece. Cut the cabbage into the thinnest possible slices, and then chop the slices until they are about 2 inches long. Mix the cabbage, grated carrots, and grated onion together in a medium mixing bowl.

2. In a separate bowl, mix together the mayonnaise, sour cream, vinegar, oil, salt, sugar, and optional celery seed with a spoon until it is just combined. Pour this dressing over the cabbage mixture and mix it together with your fingers until it is evenly coated. Refrigerate until ready to use.

Fried New Potatoes

Makes 8 servings

Kind of a cross between a French fry and a home fry, these potatoes could become one of your favorite side dishes. Don't let the kids taste them or you'll be cooking them all the time.

2 pounds small red new potatoes, rinsed and the flecks of dirt wiped off

2 cups (approximately) vegetable oil

2 tablespoons Creole seasoning

1 teaspoon salt

Note

You can boil the potatoes earlier in the day. Drain them, pat them dry, and leave them at room temperature covered with a dishcloth or paper towel for up to 3 hours before frying them.

1. Cut the new potatoes into quarters and place them in a medium saucepan with enough cold water to cover and bring them to a boil over medium-high heat. When the water boils, reduce the heat to medium low and simmer the potatoes for 12 minutes. Drain the potatoes and transfer them to paper toweling. Pat them gently with more paper towels until they are dry. Spoon the creole seasoning and salt over the potatoes.

2. Heat ¾ inch of oil in a skillet over medium-high heat until the surface of the oil begins to shimmer slightly. The oil should not be smoking, however. Add half the potatoes, being very careful to lower them gently into the oil in batches using a long-handled slotted spoon. Cook the potatoes until they are golden brown, about 4 minutes. Remove them with a slotted spoon to more paper towels to drain. Let the oil heat for another 30 seconds, and then add the remaining potatoes and cook them in the same way. Serve immediately or reheat uncovered in a 300°F oven for 10 minutes.

Banana Splits with Cognac Hot Fudge

Makes 8 servings

It can't get any worse. Your team's defense is being manhandled, the secondary picked apart. The offense is sputtering. Your quarterback is sacked five times, his passes are picked off, and the front line can't open a hole large enough for a snake to slither through. Somehow, you're only down 7 in the last quarter. It's 4th and one and you're going for it. The game rests on this play. But whatever the outcome, you'll be content, because there's still a little hot fudge left in the bottom of your bowl.

8 bananas
1 quart vanilla ice cream
2 cups homemade Hot Fudge
Cognac Sauce (recipe follows)

Concentrated whipped cream
8 Maraschino cherries

1. Peel the bananas, cut them in half lengthwise, and arrange them on the sides of individual shallow bowls. Place 2 scoops of ice cream between the banana halves.

2. Top the ice cream with a healthy portion (about ¼ cup) of hot fudge. Squirt some whipped cream over the top and place a cherry in the center of the cream. Serve immediately.

Hot Fudge Cognac Sauce

Makes 1½ cups

You're going to look at your blender in a whole new way after using it to make this sauce.

½ cup half and half

½ cup cognac, brandy, or whiskey

8 ounces bittersweet chocolate, broken into pieces

¼ cup sugar

2 teaspoon vanilla extract

1. In a small saucepan, bring the half and half and the cognac to a boil over medium heat.

2. While the mixture is heating, put the chocolate, sugar, and vanilla in a blender.

3. As soon as the half and half mixture boils, remove it from the heat and pour it into the blender along with the chocolate. Cover the blender and puree until the mixture is smooth, about 20 seconds. Serve hot.

Fun and Games

After my initial fascination with the contact, the next aspect of football that excited me were the names. The kids I knew in elementary school were mostly Bills and Eds and Mikes and Andys. Granted, football had its share of commonplace names. But there were others that seemed uniquely designed to sound like football players, whose parents must have had some prenatal premonition that their son's name would be called over a loud speaker to the roaring appreciation of 100,000 fans. Names like Butkus, Nitchky, and Katcavage.

These are my favorite football names. Some were great players. Some just had great monickers. You can add your own to the list. When you say them, you have to do it with gusto, with the raw intensity of a linebacker meeting a fullback head on at the line of scrimmage.

Sam Huff

Erich Barnes

Big Daddy Lipscomb

Dick Mojalevski

Homer Jones

Ray Nitschky

Del Shafner

Dick "Night Train" Lane

King Hill

Jim Katcavage

Lance Renthrow

Dick Butkus

Y. A. Tittle

Jim Brown

Larry Csonka

Kyle Rote

Index